Why can't computer books be easier to understand?

Not all of us want to become computer professionals, but we do want to have fun with our computers and be productive. The new *Simple Guides* cover the popular topics in computing. Most importantly, they are simple to understand. Each book in the series introduces the main features of a topic and shows you how to get the most from your PC.

Simple Guides – No gimmicks, no jargon, no fuss

Available in the *Simple Guides* series:

The Internet

Searching the Internet

The PC

Office 2000

Windows 98

E-commerce

Digital cameras, scanning and using images

Internet research

Building a website

Creating and using spreadsheets

Using email

Putting audio and video on your website

Writing for your website

Dreamweaver 4

A simple guide to

digital cameras, scanning and using images

Mary Lojkine

An imprint of PEARSON EDUCATION

Pearson Education Limited

Head Office:
Edinburgh Gate
Harlow
Essex CM20 2JE
Tel: +44 (0)1279 623623
Fax: +44 (0)1279 431059

London Office:
128 Long Acre
London WC2E 9AN
Tel: +44 (0)20 7447 2000
Fax: +44 (0)20 7240 5771
website: www.it-minds.com

First published in Great Britain in 2001
© Pearson Education Limited 2001

ISBN 0-130-93876-9

The right of Mary Lojkine to be identified
as the author of this work has been asserted by her in accordance
with the Copyright, Designs and Patents Act 1988.

British Library Cataloguing-in-Publication Data
A catalogue record for this book can be obtained from the British Library.

10 9 8 7 6 5 4 3 2 1

Typeset by Pantek Arts Ltd, Maidstone, Kent.
Printed and bound in Italy.

The publishers' policy is to use paper manufactured from sustainable forests.

Contents

7 Image editing 117

8 Selective changes 135

11 Choosing a printer

Introduction

This book provides a simple guide to digital imaging. It explains how to get images on to your computer, how to edit them, and how to use them – both on the internet and in printed material. It was written with three groups of people in mind: computer users, photographers, and complete beginners.

A simple guide for computer users

You've been using personal computers for a while, you know your way around Windows, you'd rather use a word processor than write letters by hand, and you're probably connected to the internet. You might not consider yourself a computer expert, but you're comfortable behind a keyboard.

Now you want to purchase a digital camera or scanner so you can add photographs to your documents and e-mail them to your friends. You know you can do this – and much more – but you aren't sure what you need or how to use it. This book will help you choose the right hardware and software. It also covers the basics of photography. With a few seconds' thought before you press the shutter button, you can avoid hours of work on the computer.

A simple guide for photographers

Alternatively, you might be a keen photographer. You understand shutter speeds and apertures, but computers are a mystery. Nevertheless, you know digital imaging is the coming thing, because your favourite camera shop has been overrun by digital cameras, scanners, memory cards, cables, printers, ink cartridges and special papers. Now you want to know what all the fuss is about.

This book won't turn you into a computer whiz, but it does explain what computers can do. It shows you how to set up a 'digital darkroom' and helps you mimic traditional retouching and printing techniques. You'll also find out about new ways to use your photographs once they're on your computer.

A simple guide for complete beginners

If you're new to computers *and* photography, you might be feeling overwhelmed. Don't be. Because this book was written partly for people who don't know much about photography and partly for people who don't know much about computers, it also caters for people who don't know much about either.

If you need help choosing a computer, installing software and organising your files, investigate the other books in this series. *A Simple Guide to the PC* and *A Simple Guide to Windows 98* will get you started.

Icons

These notes provide additional information about the subject concerned.

These notes indicate a variety of shortcuts: keyboard shortcuts, additional options, techniques reserved for experts, and so on.

A digital darkroom

Doing more with your photos

Digital imaging in three easy steps

Try before you buy

Setting up a digital darkroom

Digital imaging is an exciting new technology that helps you make the most of your photographs. It lets you edit them on your computer and use them in many different ways: in documents, on the internet, on cards and calendars, and even on gifts such as mugs and T-shirts.

Another advantage is speed. With a digital camera, you can see something interesting one minute and send out pictures of it the next. Digital imaging makes one-hour photo labs seem pedestrian – and expensive. The third benefit is that you can take lots of photos without worrying about the cost.

Doing more with your photos

Suppose you have a photograph of a parrot (Figure 1.1). In the normal order of things, you take a quick look and decide how it turned out. If you're pleased with it, you stick it in your album. If you aren't impressed with it, it might end up in a shoebox under your bed. Or maybe you just throw it out.

With digital imaging, you have many more choices (Figure 1.2). You can:

- edit the image to remove the red parrot from the background
- insert the parrot into another photograph to make a new image
- e-mail the photograph to a parrot-loving friend
- make a parrot logo to use on your website
- create a calendar to hang in your kitchen
- make your own, unique, parrot T-shirt.

When you take a conventional photograph, your creative input ends when you press the shutter button (unless you have a darkroom, but these days few people

Figure 1.1 This parrot photograph was taken with a conventional camera.

develop their own films). With digital imaging, taking the picture is just the beginning. A single shot can be adapted for several different projects, so you get more mileage out of your best pictures. What's more, it costs nothing to experiment.

Digital imaging also makes it easy to share photographs. If you have access to the internet, you can e-mail snapshots to friends and relatives in minutes. You don't have to finish the film, have it developed, choose the best shots, order reprints, find an envelope, and post off the pictures.

Figure 1.2 Digital imaging lets you do more with your photographs.

You can share your photographs with a wider audience by displaying them on the world wide web. Alternatively, you might already have a website dedicated to your hobbies, interests, travels, or job. Photographs of people and places are more interesting than wordy descriptions, so adding images will help to bring your website to life.

Digital imaging in three easy steps

What exactly does digital imaging involve? Basically, it involves working with photographs on a personal computer. It covers everything from taking photographs with a digital camera to editing images on the computer to printing pictures that you've captured, created or downloaded from the internet. If you have photographs in one hand and a mouse in the other, you're probably engaged in some form of digital imaging.

Digital imaging can be broken down into three areas:

- capture: getting images on to the computer
- editing: using the computer to manipulate the images
- output: getting the images off the computer.

Image capture

Imagine you're standing on the rim of the Grand Canyon. You could admire the view for hours, but your tour bus is about to leave, so you settle for capturing an image that you can work with on your computer. You have two options:

- Take a photograph with a digital camera.
- Take a photograph with a regular camera, then use a scanner to convert it into a computer file.

A digital camera looks much like a regular camera and is operated the same way: you point it at something and press the shutter button (Figure 1.3). The difference is that a digital camera doesn't use film. Instead, it records the scene as a computer file. When you get home, you can transfer the file to your computer and display the Grand Canyon on your monitor.

If you use a regular camera, you'll have to get the film developed before you can create a computer version of your Grand Canyon image. When you get your pictures back, you can place the photograph on a scanner – a device that looks like a small photocopier (Figure 1.4). The scanner examines the photograph and creates a computer file that duplicates the scene.

Digital cameras and scanners are different tools for doing the same job: getting photographs on to your computer. You only need one or the other, although you might choose to have both. Digital cameras are great when you want to get photographs on to your computer as quickly as possible. Scanners are cheaper and make more sense if you already have lots of conventional camera gear and a stack of prints you want to edit.

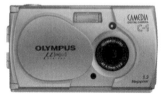

Figure 1.3 Olympus' Camedia C-1 looks like a film camera, but records images digitally.

Figure 1.4 The Astra 3450 scanner from UMAX has the lift-up lid and glass plate of a small photocopier.

Image editing

Once your photographs are on your computer, you can view them on the screen. However, there's more to digital imaging than using your computer as a very expensive photo frame. You can also use an image-editing program to make changes to your photos, either to correct problems or to make the photographs more suitable for a particular project.

You'll probably start by making overall improvements. For example, you can change the brightness and contrast (in photography terms, adjust the exposure) to give the image more punch. You can also correct the colour balance, make a photograph softer or sharper, or crop it to make the main subject more prominent (Figure 1.5).

If you develop your own photographs, you'll know you can do all these things in a traditional darkroom (if you rely on one-hour photo labs, the operator does most of them for you). The advantage of using a computer is that you don't need chemicals. Nor do you have to work in the dark.

Figure 1.5 Image editing can make your photograph (a) more like the scene you remember (b).

The next thing you might do is change some of the details. For example, suppose your photograph of the Grand Canyon includes a walker in a bright red jacket. If he spoils the picture, you can edit him out. Likewise, telegraph poles erupting from people's heads and TV aerials poking up from picturesque cottages can be magically removed.

Alternatively, you could completely transform the photograph. Imaging-editing programs can make it look like a painting or drawing, or turn it into a mosaic, or show you how the scene would look through textured glass. These effects are useful when you want a more abstract image (Figure 1.6).

Figure 1.6 Turn your photograph (a) into a painting (b) for a softer effect.

It's also possible to combine two or more photographs into a single image. The simplest example is a panorama made from two photographs that overlap. Instead of putting both pictures in your album and expecting people to ignore the joins, you can combine them into a single, seamless image.

A more challenging task is to combine elements from two unrelated photographs. The classic example is the missing relative at a big wedding (perhaps she was visiting the Grand Canyon?). If you have a suitable picture from another event, you can add her to the back row of the group photograph. Or if you're looking for a humorous shot, you could paste in a couple of politicians, a pair of pirates and a parrot.

Some people believe that using a computer to produce 'pseudophotographs' is contrary to the spirit of photography. It certainly makes you think twice about phrases such as 'capture the moment' and 'the camera never lies'. However, image editing doesn't have to be about creating impossible scenes. It can simply be a tool for getting the best out of your photographs.

Image output
Stacking up image files on your computer is like keeping snapshots in a shoe-box under your bed – they're out of sight, and mostly out of mind. To share your pictures with other people, you need to get the images off your computer. There are two options for doing this:

- use a colour printer to print your photographs.
- share your images online, either by e-mail or via the web.

Modern colour printers produce photographs that are almost indistinguishable from prints from a one-hour lab (Figure 1.7). The main difference is the feel of the paper. Once your prints are in a frame or album, no one need know that they aren't 'real' photographs. If you want pictures to hand round informally or hang on your wall, a colour printer is the answer.

However, one of the main attractions of digital imaging is that you can share your images electronically. If you have access to the internet, you don't need any special equipment to e-mail photographs to your friends. It's also easy to display them on the world wide web. There are websites that enable you to show off your images, or you can create web pages of your own (Figure 1.8).

Figure 1.7 Colour printers such as Hewlett-Packard's DeskJet 950C produce high-quality output.

Figure 1.8 Show off your best photographs on the web.

Try before you buy

Digital imaging is a lot of fun, but it can also be expensive and time consuming. If you aren't sure whether it's something you'll enjoy, investigate Kodak's Picture CD service. It provides a gentle introduction, enabling you to experiment with a few image files before you spend a lot of money on special equipment.

Buy a roll of film and take some pictures with your existing camera (if you don't have one, a disposable camera will do). Take the film into your local photo lab and ask if it offers the Picture CD service – most labs do. About a week later you'll be able to pick up your prints, plus a CD-ROM containing a digital version of each shot (Figure 1.9). The CD also has software that enables you to view and modify the images, e-mail them to your friends and print them out.

Figure 1.9 Try your hand at digital imaging with Kodak's Picture CD service (a, b).

Picture CD only gives you a taste of digital imaging, but it's an easy way to get started. You don't need a digital camera, a scanner, image-editing software or even a printer. However, you do need a computer. If that's something you're still thinking about, find a friend who's into digital imaging and ask for a demonstration. Most photographers are more than happy to show off their toys.

Setting up a digital darkroom

Exactly what you'll need in your digital darkroom depends on what you want to do, but here's a basic checklist:

- digital camera and/or scanner
- computer
- image-editing software
- colour printer and/or access to the internet.

The choice between a digital camera and a scanner depends on a number of factors, including cost, speed, flexibility, the type of photography you do and your investment in conventional camera gear. The pros and cons of both options are covered in Chapters 3 and 5.

A computer is essential, and you'll need one that's reasonably powerful. A picture is not only worth a thousand words but also, from a computer's point of view, a thousand times more work. If your system isn't up to the job, you'll find everything happens...very...slowly...and you may not be able to edit or print your images. An ideal computer for editing images would have:

- the fastest processor currently available
- at least 128Mb of RAM (memory), and maybe more
- a hard disk with 10–20Gb of free space
- a 17- or 19-inch colour monitor
- a graphics card running in True Color mode
- a CD-ROM drive, a keyboard and a mouse.

Don't panic if your computer doesn't meet these requirements. With patience, you can edit images on a computer that has:

- a Pentium-class processor
- 32Mb of RAM (64Mb would be better)
- a hard disk with 2–5Gb of free space
- a colour monitor
- a graphics card running in High Color mode
- a CD-ROM drive, a keyboard and a mouse.

If you've bought your computer in the last couple of years, it probably falls somewhere between these two sets of requirements. The most important factors are the amount of memory and the graphics card. Fortunately, both these items can be upgraded. Ask your supplier for advice.

As your image collection grows, the files may take over your hard disk. A CD writer or Zip drive enables you to offload them on to CD-ROMs or high-capacity disks (Figure 1.10). These devices are also useful when you want to

*To find out how much memory you have, click the **Start** button and select **Settings**, then **Control Panel**. Double-click on the **System** icon (you may need to click 'view all Control Panel options' to make it visible). The amount of memory in your computer is displayed in the General section of the dialogue box.*

Figure 1.10 Iomega's Zip drives enable you to store image files on 100 or 250 Mb disks.

*To find out which mode your graphics card is using, right-click on the Windows desktop and select **Properties** from the pop-up menu. Click the **Settings** tab. Look at the **Colors** option. Can you set it to **High Color** or (ideally) **True Color**?*

send images to other people. Putting a disk in the mail can be more practical than e-mailing a large image or a large collection of smaller ones.

Programs for editing digital photographs vary enormously in both price and power. Some are designed for beginners and lead you through various projects, providing guidance at every step (Figure 1.11). Others offer more powerful tools, but expect you to work out how to use them by yourself. They focus on photo editing, leaving you to dream up your own projects. Chapter 7 helps you choose the right software.

If you only want to e-mail pictures to your friends or add photographs to your website, you won't need a printer. Once you start editing your images, you'll probably want physical prints as well. Even then, a printer isn't essential, because many photo labs can print digital images. Having your own printer is simply more convenient. Chapter 11 tells you what to look for.

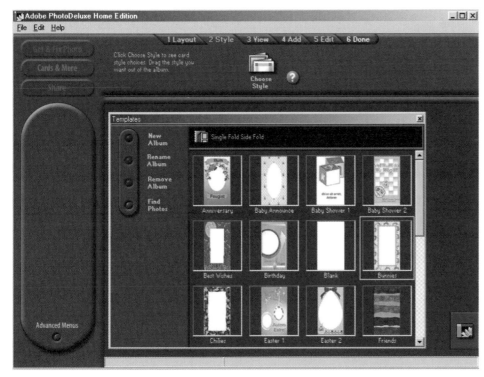

Figure 1.11 Adobe PhotoDeluxe helps you turn your photographs into cards.

—

Images on the computer

2

Before you go shopping for equipment and software, you should learn how computers handle images. With a little knowledge tucked away, you won't be baffled when enthusiastic salespeople start raving about terms such as 'megapixels' and 'compressed images'.

This chapter provides the technical background for the rest of the book. Don't worry if you don't understand everything straight away, because you can come back to it when you need a refresher. Some of the principles are easier to grasp when you've seen them in action.

Pixels

Most people think computers are clever and complicated. In reality, they are simple and stupid. They're only useful because they can do lots of simple, stupid things very quickly.

Take the parrot photograph from Chapter 1 (Figure 2.1). To you, it's clearly a picture of a parrot. You might recognise it as a blue and yellow macaw. You might think it looks cross. You can easily hold the whole image in your head.

A computer can't deal with photographs in such a sophisticated way. Instead, it breaks them down into thousands of tiny dots, arranged in rows and columns. Each dot is a single colour. It's as if the computer is recreating the image on an enormous piece of graph paper, by colouring in individual squares.

When you look at a photograph on the computer screen, you can't see the dots. However, if you magnify a small area of the image, you stop seeing parrot and start seeing coloured squares (Figure 2.2). These are the dots that the computer works with.

Figure 2.1 It's that parrot again…

Each dot is properly known as a 'picture element' or 'pixel'. To store the image, the computer records the colour of each pixel, so across the centre of the parrot's eye you might get something like 'light-green pixel, mid-green pixel, grey pixel, black pixel, black pixel, black pixel' and so on.

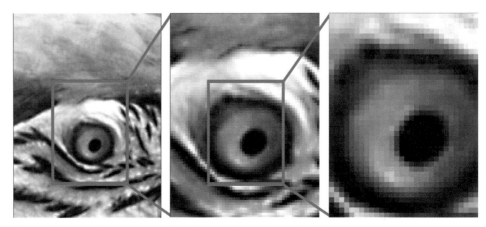

Figure 2.2 a–c To a computer, this photograph is just a grid of dots.

Resolution

Colouring in squares is not the best way to produce an image with smooth curves. As you can see from Figure 2.2c, what you actually get is jagged zigzags. The way round this is to make the pixels very small, so you can't see their edges. Of course, this means you need plenty of them.

The 'resolution' of an image tells you how many pixels it contains, how small they are, and how smooth the curves will be. Strictly speaking, it should be measured on a per-inch basis. So, if your picture is three inches wide, and a line across it contains 900 pixels, it has a resolution of 300 pixels per inch (900 ÷ 3). Because pixels are just dots, it's normal to write this as '300 dots per inch', or '300 dpi' (Figure 2.3).

← ———— 3 inches, 900 pixels ————— →

Resolution

= 900 pixels ÷ 3 inches

= 300 dots per inch

Figure 2.3 To calculate the resolution, divide the width by the number of pixels.

Pixels are square, so it doesn't matter whether you count them horizontally, across the top of the image, or vertically, down the side. Either way, you'll get 300dpi. Think about coloured squares on graph paper again, and you'll see what this means. If you take a square inch of the image, you have 300 rows of pixels, and each row contains 300 pixels. In total, you have 90 000 pixels (300 × 300). As you can imagine, they are pretty small, so your eyes blend them together to create a smooth, pixel-free image (Figure 2.4).

Personal computers were developed in the United States, where they still use imperial measurements. And photographers measure film in millimetres, but order prints in inches. This book sticks with the most commonly accepted units, however illogical they may be.

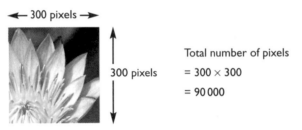

← 300 pixels →

300 pixels

Total number of pixels

= 300 × 300

= 90 000

Figure 2.4 A 300 dpi image has 90 000 pixels per square inch.

Typical resolutions

A computer monitor displays images at somewhere between 72 and 100 dpi, depending on how it is set up. This is quite a low resolution and if you get close enough to the screen, you can make out the individual pixels in a digital photograph. From a normal viewing distance, though, it looks fine. The points of coloured light blend together, giving a smooth, attractive image.

If you print an image at 72 dpi, it doesn't look so good (Figure 2.5a). When the seductive glow of the monitor is removed, you see the image more clearly and you notice the rough edges. You also become more critical and expect to see all the fine details.

To match the sharpness of a conventional photograph, you need to print at 300 dpi. This is the big difference between producing images for use online, for example on a website, and producing images to be printed: printed images require a lot more pixels (Figure 2.5b).

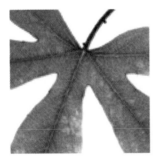

Figure 2.5 A 72 dpi image (a) looks fine on screen but terrible on paper, where 300 dpi (b) is required.

Size matters

Resolution will give you a headache, because it isn't fixed and immutable. When you change the size of a digital photograph, you change its resolution.

The computer doesn't know how big an image should be; it just knows how many pixels are stored in the file. (Remember, an image file records the colour of each pixel on the image grid.) Resolution doesn't become an issue until you want to print the image, or use it on a website. You then have to decide how big it should be.

Suppose you have an 600 × 450-pixel file (Figure 2.6).

- If you make the image two inches wide, the resolution is 300 dpi. Each square inch contains 90 000 invisibly small pixels.
- If you make it three inches wide, the resolution is 200 dpi. Each square inch contains 40 000 pixels that are still pretty small.

Figure 2.6 This image is 600 pixels wide, and 450 tall.

- If you make it ten inches wide, the resolution is 60 dpi. Each square inch contains 360 quite large pixels that are fairly easy to see.
- If you make it 100 inches wide, the resolution is 6 dpi. Each square inch contains 36 enormous pixels that are impossible to miss.

The computer lets you print this image any size you want. However, if you want it to look like a photograph, rather than a grid of coloured squares, you have to keep it quite small (Figure 2.7).

Adding and removing pixels

There's a further twist: as well as changing the size of the image, you can change the number of pixels in the image file. This also affects the resolution.

To reduce the number of pixels, the computer goes through the file and throws out some of the information. Voilà, fewer pixels.

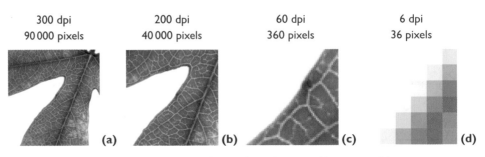

300 dpi	200 dpi	60 dpi	6 dpi
90 000 pixels	40 000 pixels	360 pixels	36 pixels
(a)	(b)	(c)	(d)

Figure 2.7a–d As you enlarge an image, the pixels get bigger and become visible.

Adding pixels is more complicated. The computer looks at each group of pixels, averages their colours, and inserts extra pixels of intermediate colours. Voilà, more pixels. This process is called 'interpolation'.

The main reason for removing pixels is to reduce the amount of information you have to store. You end up with a smaller file that takes up less room on your hard disk and is easier to work with. If you are using it on the web, it downloads more quickly.

You should only add pixels as a last resort. Because the computer is simply inventing new pixels based on the ones you already have, interpolation doesn't add detail to the image, and it can make it look fuzzy. If you have a sharp divide between a black area and a white area, the computer adds a row of grey pixels, softening the edge. However, if you have to print a file at a certain size, and it simply doesn't have enough pixels, made-up pixels are better than nothing (Figure 2.8).

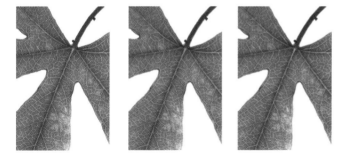

Figure 2.8 Here's the 300 dpi leaf again (a). The computer can throw away pixels, bringing the resolution down to 150 dpi (b). It can then add pixels to bring the resolution back to 300 dpi (c), but it can't recreate the fine detail.

Megapixels

The problem with expressing resolution in the traditional way (as the number of dots per inch) is that you have to know two things:

- the number of pixels in your file
- the size of the image when it's printed.

If you're manufacturing a digital camera, you know how many pixels it will capture, because this depends on the sensor inside it. However, you don't know whether the person who buys it is going to print 6 × 4-inch snapshots or 10 × 8-inch enlargements, so you can't talk about pixels per inch. Instead, you calculate the number of pixels *per image*.

Suppose your digital camera takes 1600 × 1200-pixel photographs. This gives you 1 920 000 pixels per image. That's an unwieldy number, so you write it as 1.9 million pixels. Except that doesn't sound very technical, so you use the scientific term for million, 'mega'. Now you have a 1.9-megapixel image, so you tell people your camera has a resolution of 1.9 megapixels (Figure 2.9).

Resolutions measured in megapixels behave differently from resolutions measured in dots per inch. When you use megapixels, you're counting the dots in an area. When you use dots per inch, you're counting across a line. This leads to all sorts of confusion (see page 48). It would be better if camera manufacturers had picked a different term, but for now you're stuck with two meanings for 'resolution'.

When in doubt, concentrate on the measurements that brook no argument: the width and height of the image, in pixels. These figures are the key to everything else.

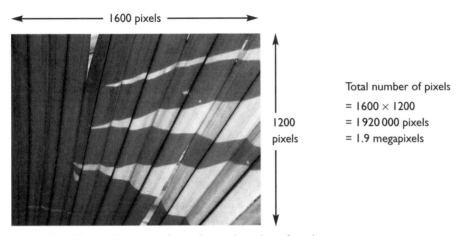

◄——————— 1600 pixels ———————►

1200
pixels

Total number of pixels
= 1600 × 1200
= 1 920 000 pixels
= 1.9 megapixels

Figure 2.9 Megapixel ratings refer to the total number of pixels.

Five things to remember
Resolution can be an exasperating concept. However, it's worth grappling with, because it affects the appearance of your digital images. Here's a quick summary of the five most important points:

- Resolution is the number of pixels per inch in the final image.
- For an image to look good on the screen, you need a resolution of 72 dpi.
- For it to look perfect on paper, you need a resolution of 300 dpi.
- You can change the resolution by changing the size of the printed image.
- You can also change the resolution by adding or removing pixels.

Finding the optimum resolution for your images is an important step in any digital imaging project. If the resolution is too low, they won't look good. However, that doesn't mean you should crank up the resolution as high as possible. Having more pixels than you need slows down your computer, because it has to process unnecessary information. You want the resolution to be just right.

Colours

Now you've counted your pixels, you can assign colours. How many shades will you need? (Remember, each pixel can only be one colour.) Hundreds? Thousands? In fact, the answer is millions. The human eye is very perceptive, so you need lots of different colours to create smooth transitions between various shades (Figure 2.10).

Figure 2.10 This image contains just 256 colours, so the transitions between colours are obvious.

Colours on the screen

Monitors make colours by mixing red, green and blue light. Each pixel on your screen consists of three tiny glowing dots, one of each colour. When all three dots are turned off, you get a black pixel. When they're turned on at full strength, you get a white pixel.

To make other colours, the computer turns on the three dots at different levels. For example, if the red and green dots are on at full strength, and the blue dot is off, you get yellow. If red is at full strength, green at half strength and blue off, you get orange, and so on. (If these combinations sound strange, it's because mixing light is the opposite of mixing ink – everything works backwards.) This system for creating colours is called the 'RGB' system.

To get all the different shades required for a photographic image, the computer has to be able to set each dot to 256 different levels, ranging from fully off to fully on. It can then combine the 256 red settings with the 256 green settings and the 256 blue settings to produce 16.7 million different colours – more than you can see. This way of doing things is called '24-bit colour' or 'True Color'.

Computers don't always operate in True Color mode. Most of the time you don't need millions of colours, so you can get by with fewer intensity levels for each dot. Your computer might be operating in High Color mode, which gives you 65 536 possible colours, or even 256-colour mode. However, True Color mode is best for digital imaging.

To check the colour mode, and change it if necessary:

1. Right-click on the Windows desktop.
2. Select **Properties** from the pop-up menu.

In computing, the smallest unit of information is called a 'bit'. It takes eight bits to store a number between zero and 255 (giving you 256 settings, when you include zero). To store the red, blue and green settings for an individual pixel, you need 24 bits.

3. Click the **Settings** tab.

4. Change the **Colors** setting to **True Color** (Figure 2.11).

5. Click **OK**.

6. You may be prompted to restart your computer. If so, save your work and click **OK**.

Printed colours

A printer makes colours with inks rather than light, so it uses a different mixing scheme.

Most colour printers use four inks: cyan, magenta, yellow and black (often abbreviated to 'CMYK'). In an ideal world, only three would be necessary, because cyan, magenta and yellow should combine to make black. In practice, you get dark brown, so black ink is used as well.

Cyan, magenta and yellow are the complements of red, blue and green, and they mix together in a similar (but less confusing) way. Cyan plus magenta gives you blue, cyan plus yellow gives you green, and magenta plus yellow gives you red.

When you print a file, the computer automatically converts the red, blue and green information in the file to the cyan, magenta, yellow and black information that the printer requires (Figure 2.12). You don't have to do anything, which is a blessing. However, you may notice that very bright greens look darker on printouts than they do on the screen. There are a few colours that the CMYK system can't reproduce.

Most printers don't actually 'mix' colours. Instead, they lay down patterns of tiny dots. For example, to make red, they print magenta and yellow dots. From a

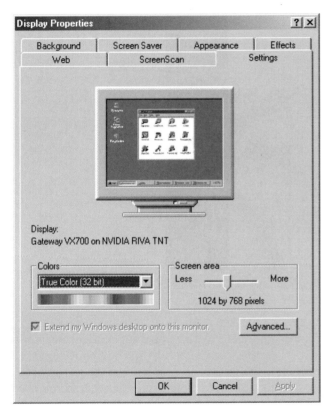

Figure 2.11 The Display Properties dialogue box tells you which colour mode your computer is using.

When you were at school, you probably made colours by mixing red, blue and yellow paint. This works well in art classes, but it makes science teachers weep. When you want photo-realistic colours, the laws of physics get their revenge. If you're working with light, the primary colours are red, green and blue. When you print, they are cyan, magenta and yellow.

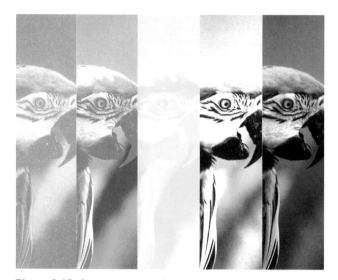

Figure 2.12 Printers use tiny dots of cyan, magenta, yellow and black ink to create all the colours required in a photograph.

normal viewing distance, your eye blends the dots together and you see a red shape. In other words, the small pixels you've been thinking about since the beginning of this chapter are recreated using even smaller dots when you print. It can take 16 or more printer dots to render each pixel in the image, so you need a printer resolution of at least 1200 dpi to get the best out of a 300 dpi image.

File formats

Any image file is basically just a record of the colour of each pixel in the image. However, there are several ways to store this information, giving rise to a number of 'formats' for image files. Some were designed for a specific purpose, such as use on the internet. Others belong to a particular program.

Common image formats

Most image-editing programs understand a dozen or more file formats. If your image file isn't in the right format, you can open it, then save it again, choosing a different format (Figure 2.13). Here are a few of the common formats:

- BMP (bitmap). This format is used for Windows wallpaper. It isn't much good for anything else because the files tend to be very large.
- GIF (Graphics Interchange Format). This format is unusual in that images can only contain 256 colours. It is often used on the web for logos and illustrations, but isn't suitable for photographs.
- JPEG or JPG (Joint Photographic Experts Group). This True Color (24-bit) format was developed for photographs. It uses image compression (see below) to create compact files that can be transmitted by e-mail or used on websites.
- PSD (Photoshop document). This is an example of a format that belongs to a particular program – in this case, Adobe Photoshop. It stores extra information used by some of Photoshop's special tools.

*If your filenames don't end with a dot, followed by three letters, you need to make the file endings (or 'extensions') visible. Run Windows Explorer, then go to the **Tools** menu and select **Folder Options**. Click the **View** tab. Deselect the **Hide file extensions for known file types** checkbox (in other words, click it to remove the tick), then click **OK**.*

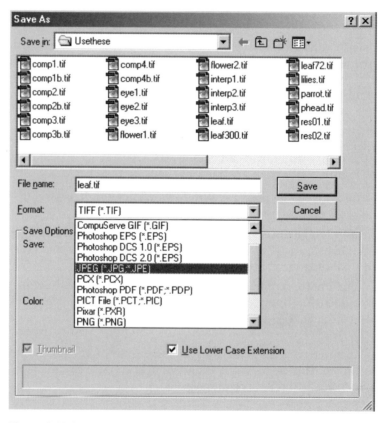

Figure 2.13 Image-editing programs offer a selection of image formats.

■ TIFF or TIF (Tagged Image File Format). This is the favourite format of the desktop publishing community. It comes in many variations and is often used for photographs. However, TIFF files can't be used on the web. They are too large and web browsers don't know how to display them.

You can deduce the format of an image file from the three letters that appear at the end of the filename. These three letters are known as a file 'extension'. For example, mypic.jpg is a JPEG.

Image compression

From a digital photographer's point of view, the main difference between image formats is that some store information *efficiently*, while others store it more *accurately*. Efficient storage is important when you are using photographs on the internet, because it leads to small files that download quickly. Accurate storage is important when you want the best possible print quality.

Compression is the key to efficiency. At its simplest, it involves condensing the information in the file. Instead of writing, 'blue pixel, blue pixel, blue pixel, blue pixel, blue pixel, white pixel, white pixel', the computer writes 'five blue pixels, two white pixels'. This is known as 'lossless' compression, because you don't lose any information.

If you want to make the file even smaller, you have to throw away some of the information it contains. Suppose you have an area of blue sky. Probably the pixels vary slightly in colour, but no one will notice if you make them all the same colour. This is how the JPEG format compresses images. It divides the pixels into blocks, then simplifies each block so it can be stored more compactly. At low levels of compression, you don't notice the changes, because you're just losing random variations in tone. At higher levels, the simplifications become greater, and you start to see 'artifacts' in the photograph – areas that look 'blocky', or have gone strange colours. This is called 'lossy' compression, because you lose some of the detail in your image (Figure 2.14).

Compression is essential when you're preparing images for use online (see Chapter 9). However, it is a compromise. Overdo the compression and you'll spoil your images.

Figure 2.14 Compare these images with no compression (a), low compression (b), high compression (c) and far too much compression (d).

Choosing a digital camera

3

Compared to computers, digital cameras are easy to understand. You point the lens, you press the button, you see your picture on the built-in screen. It's the ultimate in instant gratification.

A digital camera can change the way you take pictures. Not sure if a shot will come out? Try it. If it doesn't work, delete it and try again. Want to know what's wrong with your houseplants? Instead of describing the problem, e-mail a picture to a green-fingered friend (Figure 3.1). When you're freed from the twin tyrannies of finishing the film and paying for the prints, photographs are a convenient way to communicate.

How do digital cameras work?

A digital camera is just a regular camera with a bunch of electronics where the film should be. The lens focuses light on to an image sensor, which converts the light into electrical signals. The camera's processor turns these signals into an image file, which is stored on a memory card. When you want to transfer the pictures to your computer, you connect the camera to it with a cable. Alternatively, you can remove the memory card and place it in a special reader.

Most digital cameras have a small liquid-crystal display (LCD) on the back (Figure 3.2). This enables you to review each picture as you take it. If the subject's eyes are closed or the flash didn't go off, you can delete the picture. This removes it from the camera's memory, as if it had never been taken. The LCD can also be used to display camera settings, or it can operate as a viewfinder.

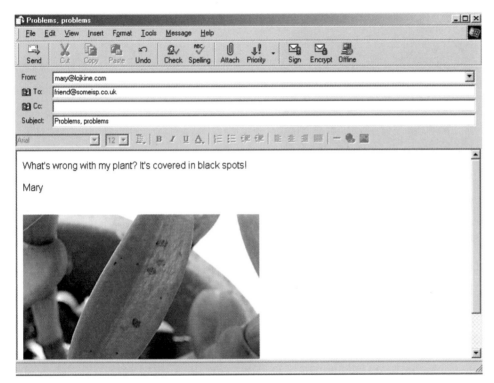

Figure 3.1 Why struggle with a description when you can send a picture?

Figure 3.2 The LCD on the back of Olympus' Camedia C-3040 ZOOM camera displays the picture you're about to take, or the one you've just taken.

Pros and cons

Digital cameras are great, but they aren't for everyone. Depending on your interests, you might be better off with a film camera and a scanner (see Chapter 5).

Digital cameras give you instant feedback and immediate access to your images. Mistakes don't matter, because there are no processing costs. You only pay for the images you want to print, and printing images at home is (slightly) cheaper than ordering reprints. The latest digital cameras match the image quality of 35 mm compact cameras. They also have extra features such as the ability to record sound and short video clips.

However, digital cameras are several times more expensive than comparable film cameras. They are larger and heavier, and require a lot more power. If you use ordinary batteries, you'll be replacing them constantly. If you use rechargeable ones, you'll always have half an eye on the nearest power socket. Digital cameras store images on expensive memory cards rather than cheap, readily available film. This means you have to offload your pictures on to a computer at regular intervals, which is awkward when you're away from home. Accessories are specialised and expensive.

For the same money, a single-lens reflex (SLR) camera with interchangeable lenses lets you take a wider range of pictures. A digital camera gives you images more quickly.

The best digital camera

If you walk into a shop and ask to see the 'best' digital camera, the assistant will steer you towards the newest and most expensive model. Or, if you're very lucky and ask someone unusually conscientious, they'll spend the next hour asking you questions such as, 'What do you want to photograph?' and 'What will you do with the images?'

There is no 'best' camera. There isn't even a best camera in a particular price range. There are just cameras that are good at particular things, or for certain types of people.

Digital cameras are more diverse than regular cameras, because the technology is still evolving. Everyone has different ideas and no one is sure what people really want. A cheap camera that's easy to use? A digital camera that looks and feels like a traditional model? A tiny camera that can be taken everywhere? A high-tech camera (Figure 3.3) that beeps and whistles? A durable camera (Figure 3.4) that isn't bothered by dust or bad weather? All these cameras are available, but they won't all be right for you.

Figure 3.3 Sony's Cyber-shot DSC-F505V has a radical design dominated by a large, swivelling lens.

Figure 3.4 Kodak's DC5000 is rugged and weatherproof.

To find your own, personal 'best' camera, think about the pictures you're planning to take. Are they mostly casual snapshots of family and friends? Or do you have a special interest in close-ups, wildlife, landscapes, sports or travel photography? Second, decide whether you're going to use the images online, at low resolution, or print them out. Once you know what you want to do, you can work out what you need.

Camera features

There are lots of things to think about when you're choosing a digital camera, such as:

- lens
- sensor
- memory
- LCD/viewfinder
- standard camera features
- creative controls
- novelty features
- performance
- ergonomics
- battery
- connections
- software.

Lens

The lens creates the photograph by focusing light on to the sensor, so it's a key component. Cheap lenses are made of plastic, better ones of glass. Cheap lenses also tend to be fixed-focus. This means the lens is designed so that everything from a person standing opposite you to a tree on the horizon comes out reasonably sharp. For better results, get an auto-focus lens that automatically adjusts itself so the main subject of your photograph is as sharp as possible.

The sensors used in digital cameras are much smaller than a frame of 35 mm film, so the lenses are different. To make life easier, manufacturers compare them to the lenses on standard film cameras. If you see something like, 'Focal length 7.1 mm, equivalent to 38 mm on a 35 mm camera,' you'll get the same angle of view as a person using a film camera with a 38 mm lens.

Cheaper cameras offer a single focal length, typically equivalent to around 35 mm. More expensive ones have zoom lenses that let you increase the focal length, bringing your subject closer (Figure 3.5). The most basic option is a two times (2×) zoom that lets you change the focal length from 35 to 70 mm. There are also cameras with 3×, 4×, 5×, 6× and even monster 10× zooms (Figure 3.6).

A zoom lens makes it easier to get close to your subject, which usually gives you a better picture. However, there are a few catches. First, if you want to photograph landscapes, it's the wide end that matters. Look for a zoom that starts at 28 or 30 mm. Second, at longer focal lengths, it's important to hold the camera steady. Most of the monster zooms have anti-shake devices ('image stabilisers') that help with this. Third, make sure you're getting an optical zoom, not a digital one. With a digital zoom, the camera takes the centre of the image and uses

The focal length of a lens determines how much of a scene you can see. A lens with a short focal length has a wide angle of view and lets you capture a whole room or the sweep of a landscape. A lens with a longer focal length cuts off the edges of the scene, but makes objects in the centre seem closer.

Figure 3.6 Canon's PowerShot Pro 90 IS has a 10× zoom with an image stabiliser.

Figure 3.5 A 35–105 mm zoom lens lets you capture the big picture (top) or the important details (bottom).

interpolation (see page 26) to enlarge it. You can just as easily do this with an image-editing program, so it isn't worth paying extra for a digital zoom.

If you're interested in close-ups, look for a camera with a macro mode. Some can focus on objects just 2 cm from the lens, enabling you to photograph coins, small toys, insects, and flowers. Another useful feature is a filter thread on the front of the lens. This enables you to use filters for special effects, or lens adaptors that extend the range of your zoom.

Sensor

The sensor is as essential as the lens. It converts the incoming light into data, enabling the camera to produce an image file.

The sensor resolution is always slightly higher than the image resolution, because data from the edges of the sensor isn't very reliable. For example, a 3.3-megapixel camera produces a 3.1-megapixel image.

There are two types of sensor: charge-coupled devices (CCDs) and complementary metal-oxide semiconductor (CMOS) sensors. In general, CCDs give better images, while CMOS sensors are cheaper and use less power. There are exceptions, though – some CMOS-based cameras produce excellent photographs.

A more important consideration is the resolution of the sensor, which tells you how many pixels the images contain. More pixels means more information, so a high-resolution (high-res) sensor captures more detail than a low-res one.

Table 3.1 lists some typical camera resolutions, along with the corresponding image size. It also shows the size of your prints if you want the best possible image quality. If quality isn't everything, you can make acceptable prints that are half as large again. Figure 3.7 shows the relative sizes of the prints.

Table 3.1   Typical camera resolutions.

Camera resolution (megapixels)	Image size (pixels)	Size of 300 dpi print (inches/centimetres)
0.3*	640 × 480	2.1 × 1.6 (5.4 × 4.1)
1.0	1152 × 864	3.8 × 2.9 (9.8 × 7.3)
2.1	1600 × 1200	5.3 × 4.0 (13.5 × 10.2)
3.3	2048 × 1536	6.8 × 5.1 (17.3 × 13.0)
4.0	2240 × 1680	7.5 × 5.6 (19.0 × 14.2)

* This resolution is often called VGA, because it has the same number of pixels as an old-fashioned VGA monitor.

If you want to output your images as standard 6 × 4-inch prints, you need at least a one-megapixel camera, and ideally a two-megapixel model. Opting for a higher resolution enables you to make good-quality enlargements.

If you plan to share your photographs by e-mail or use them on your website, you can get by with a cheap VGA camera. A 640 × 480-pixel image is more than big enough for these applications. However, what happens when you take the photograph of a lifetime? You'll want to print it out, and you'll be sorry you don't have more pixels. High-resolution cameras can be switched into a low-resolution mode when you want images to share online, but the reverse isn't true.

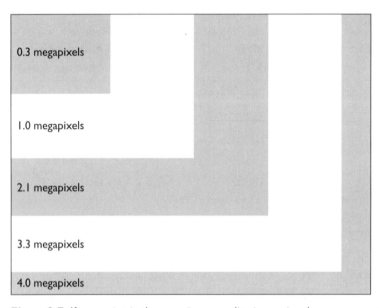

Figure 3.7 If you maintain the same image quality, increasing the camera resolution gives you larger prints.

Note that doubling the resolution of your camera doesn't double the size of your prints. This is because of the peculiar way that camera resolutions are measured (see page 28).

Finally, most digital cameras capture images that are squarer than photographs from a conventional camera. With a 35 mm camera, the ratio between the long and short sides is 3:2. With a digital camera, it's usually 4:3, making the image the same shape as a computer monitor or television screen (Figure 3.8).

Figure 3.8 A digital photograph (a) is squarer than a conventional one (b).

Memory
Most digital cameras store your image files on removable memory cards. A few of the cheaper models have built-in memory, but this is a less flexible option. Once the built-in memory is full, you have to transfer the files to your computer before you can take any more pictures. With removable memory, you can take out the full card and replace it with an empty one. You can also purchase bigger cards that hold more pictures.

There are two common types of memory cards: CompactFlash and SmartMedia (Figure 3.9). They are incompatible – you can't use a CompactFlash card in a camera designed for SmartMedia, or vice versa. CompactFlash has a slight edge if you take a lot of photographs, because it comes in larger capacities.

Alternatives include Memory Stick, which is mostly used in Sony products, and MultiMediaCard, a smaller card that's relatively little used in cameras. Some professional cameras use PC cards (also known as PCMCIA cards).

The problem with these types of memory is that they're expensive. In order to keep prices down, camera manufacturers often give you a card that's only big

Figure 3.9 Most digital cameras use either CompactFlash (a) or SmartMedia (b) memory cards. Both these cards come from SanDisk.

enough for a handful of images. This doesn't matter when you're taking pictures at home, because you can keep transferring the files to your computer. If you're going on holiday, however, you have a problem. You'll need a bigger, more expensive card.

One solution is to choose a camera that uses a cheaper storage medium, such as a floppy disk or recordable CD. These cameras are bulky, but extra memory is cheap and it's easy to transfer images to your computer – you simply put the disk or CD into your drive (Figure 3.10). Another approach is to replace your memory card with a tiny hard drive. IBM's Microdrive is the same size as a CompactFlash card, but thicker (it fits in Type II CompactFlash slots). It can hold hundreds or even thousands of images (Figure 3.11).

Figure 3.10 Sony's Mavica MVC-CD1000 records images on to an 8 cm CD-ROM.

Figure 3.11 IBM's Microdrive is a tiny hard drive. (Picture courtesy of International Business Machines Corporation. Unauthorized use not permitted.)

LCD/viewfinder

Most digital cameras have a colour LCD on the back so you can see your images as you take them.

Cheap cameras only have a small, black and white (mono) LCD. It tells you how many pictures you've taken, but can't display them. This takes a lot of the fun out of digital photography. More expensive cameras supplement the mono LCD with a colour one that lets you preview your images. This can also be used to display menus of camera options.

A colour LCD can double as a viewfinder, giving you a live preview of the image being formed by the sensor. This is handy when you're very close to your subject. A regular viewfinder doesn't show you exactly what the lens sees, because it views the scene from a different position (Figure 3.12). When you use the LCD, what you see is what you get. You can also hold the camera above your head and still have some idea what you're photographing.

Figure 3.12 The LCD on Sony's Cyber-shot DSC-S50 operates as a viewfinder, showing you exactly what the lens sees.

The downside of using the LCD as a viewfinder is that it consumes a lot of power. It's also difficult to see the image in bright sunlight. For these reasons, most cameras have a regular, optical viewfinder as well.

Standard camera features
It's easy to get so wrapped up in the special features of digital cameras that you forget about the basics. Technology is great, but it doesn't mean you can do without a flash, a self timer and a tripod mount.

You'll need a flash to take pictures indoors and to brighten up some outdoor shots. Decent cameras give you four settings: automatic, off, always on (fill flash) and anti-redeye. Some models can also be connected to an external flash.

A self-timer and a tripod mount work together, enabling you to take self portraits and sneak into group shots. A tripod mount is also useful when you need to hold the camera steady during a long exposure, such as an atmospheric night shot.

Creative controls
If you're a keen photographer, you'll want to do more than point your camera and press the shutter button. Creative controls enable you to adjust the camera settings to fine-tune the results.

To produce a correctly exposed image, the camera has to control the amount of light falling on the sensor. It does this by adjusting both the shutter speed and the aperture of the lens. These two settings can be traded off against each other.

If you use a fast shutter speed and a large aperture, you let in a lot of light for a short period of time. With a slow speed and a small aperture, the sensor gets a

A camera lens contains a diaphragm that can open and close like the iris of your eye. The size of the hole (or 'aperture') affects the amount of light that passes through and hits the camera's sensor.

trickle of light for a long period of time. The cumulative effect is identical, so both images are correctly exposed. However, they don't look the same. With a small aperture, the lens focuses light more effectively, so all the objects in your picture are sharp, regardless of their distance from the lens. With a large aperture, only the main subject is in focus (Figure 3.13).

Cameras designed for keen photographers let you make your own decisions about shutter speed and aperture. Generally they offer a shutter-priority mode, where you choose the shutter speed and the camera works out the correct aperture, and an aperture-priority mode, where the reverse happens. Some cameras also offer a full manual mode, where you choose both settings.

Figure 3.13 Switching from a small aperture (a) to a large one (b) throws the background out of focus, emphasising the flower.

Other useful options include spot metering, which enables you to tell the camera to concentrate on a small area when it's working out the exposure. For example, you might want it to expose a person's face correctly, even if this means the background is under- or overexposed.

Some cameras also let you change the sensitivity of the sensor. This is the digital camera equivalent of switching between ISO 100, 200 and 400 film. Increasing the sensitivity enables you to take pictures in poor light, but there's a trade-off in image quality. Colours aren't as bright and you get more 'noise'. Pixels that should be all the same colour end up slightly different shades, giving you a grainy effect.

Novelty features

Gong digital enables you to do things that have no parallel in the film-camera world. When you use the LCD as a viewfinder, information is transferred electronically from the sensor to the screen. Since wires can go round corners, the LCD doesn't have to be behind the lens. In fact, there's nothing stopping you from having a swivel mechanism in the middle of the camera, with the lens on one side and the screen on the other (Figure 3.14). This might seem like a gimmick, but a rotating lens is surprisingly useful. It lets you use the camera at all sorts of strange angles, including at your waist and over your head, making it easier to take candid shots.

Some digital cameras can capture sound as well as images, enabling you to make voice notes describing your location. Others let you record short video clips. The results aren't exactly broadcast quality, but they're good enough to use on a website.

Figure 3.14 The lens on Nikon's Coolpix 990 rotates through 270 degrees.

Finally, the popularity of digital music has prompted several manufacturers to produce hybrid cameras that not only take photographs, but also play music stored in the MP3 format (Figure 3.15).

Performance
When you asked about the 'best' camera on the market, you were probably looking for one that works well. There are some things you can't deduce from the information on the box, such as how quickly a camera focuses and how well it captures colours. For this kind of information, look at reviews in magazines or on the internet.

Figure 3.15 Fujifilm's FinePix 40i takes digital pictures and plays digital music.

When you're reading reviews, remember that most people are biased towards their own particular interests. Photographers favour cameras that produce great pictures, even if taking them is hard work. Computer users are more interested in the practicalities, and style magazines award points for trendy good looks. Also, a camera that's excellent at one thing may be terrible at another. Try to find reviews with a good variety of sample images, or with images that are similar to the shots you intend to take.

Ergonomics

Digital cameras come in a wide range of shapes and sizes (and a small range of colours: silver or black). Some fit comfortably into your hand, but others don't, so never buy a camera without handling it first. Ask yourself the following questions:

- Is it easy to hold, or will it slip through your fingers at the first sign of sweat?
- Can you look through the viewfinder without pressing your nose against the LCD?
- Is the shutter button easy to reach? Can you tell when you've pressed it?
- Are all the other buttons easy to press and clearly labelled?
- If there are controls that slide, twist or rock, do they click into place?
- Can you open the battery and memory-card compartments without a screw-driver? How sturdy are the flaps?
- For that matter, how sturdy is the entire camera?
- Is there a lens cap? Will you lose it?
- Can you attach a wrist or neck strap?

Battery

A film camera might run for months on a single battery, but a digital one gobbles up an entire set in hours. If you aren't careful, you can spend more on batteries than you ever did on film.

The solution is to use rechargeable batteries. More expensive cameras come with a rechargeable battery pack. Cheaper ones use standard AA batteries, but you can usually replace them with rechargeable ones (Figure 3.16). The specially designed battery packs perform better, but rechargeable AAs are more versatile. If they go flat, you can pop into any newsagent and replace them with ordinary ones.

Figure 3.16 Use rechargeable batteries to keep your costs down.

Connections

Once you've taken some pictures, you'll want to transfer them from the camera to your computer. Usually this involves connecting the two devices with a cable that plugs into the back of the computer.

There are lots of sockets on the back of your computer, but only two are relevant here (Figure 3.17):

■ Serial ports use very old technology that's slow but reliable. They're the best choice if your computer predates Windows 98 (ie Windows 95 or earlier).

■ Universal serial bus ports (USB ports) ports are much newer and enable you to transfer images more quickly. They're the better option if your computer came with Windows 98 or Windows Millennium preinstalled.

Most digital cameras only come with one type of cable. Newer cameras usually come with USB cables, whereas older cameras may be supplied with serial cables.

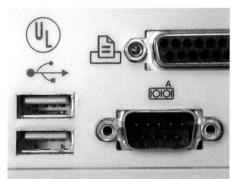  

Figure 3.17 USB ports (left) and a serial port (lower right) (a), plus a USB cable (b), and a serial cable (c).

The alternative to cables is a memory-card reader (Figure 3.18). Instead of messing about with cables, you remove the memory card from your camera and insert it into the reader, which behaves like an extra disk drive. Card readers connect to a USB port or a parallel port – a third type of socket commonly used for printers.

Some cameras also have a socket for a video cable that lets you connect the camera to a television. You can then display your images on the big screen, which is handy if you want to share them with someone who doesn't have a computer. Check that the camera outputs a PAL signal, as used in the UK.

Figure 3.18 Microtech's CameraMate reads data from CompactFlash and SmartMedia cards.

Software

You'll probably get two programs with your digital camera: one for transferring images on to the computer, and another for editing them. The trend with transfer programs is to make them as simple as possible. Some show you miniature versions of your images so you can decide which ones to copy across, but many simply treat the attached camera as an extra disk drive. The editing program is just a freebie that you can replace with another program later on (see Chapter 7).

Specialist cameras

As well as standard digital cameras, there are a couple of specialist options to consider.

Digital single-lens reflex (SLR) cameras

A single-lens reflex (SLR) camera uses a mirror to divert light from the lens up to the viewfinder, so you see exactly what the lens sees. The other advantage is that the lens can be detached from the rest of the camera. This makes SLRs very flexible. As the occasion warrants, you can replace your 28 mm wide-angle lens with a 70–200 mm zoom lens or a 600 mm telephoto lens.

There are several digital SLRs designed to work with existing lenses (Figure 3.19). This gives you the best of both worlds – but at a price. The first digital SLRs were sold to photojournalists who needed to capture high-quality images and submit them as quickly as possible. Prices have since fallen, and recent models are within reach of enthusiastic (and wealthy) amateurs.

Figure 3.19 Canon's EOS D30 digital SLR uses lenses designed for Canon's film-based cameras.

Webcams

If you take the lens and sensor of a digital camera and attach them to your computer with a long cable, you have a webcam (Figure 3.20). This is an embryonic camera that relies on the computer's processor and hard disk to capture and store images and videos.

Webcams are inexpensive, and they work well if you want low-res images of items within a few metres of your computer. For example, if you need simple mugshots for ID cards, a webcam will suffice. Another popular option is to point the camera at an interesting scene and upload snapshots to a website at regular intervals.

Figure 3.20 Logitech's QuickCam Pro is a camera on a string.

Decisions, decisions

Choosing a digital camera is about making compromises. It's easy to make a list of all the features that you would *like* to have, but you'll end up wanting a very expensive camera (or, worse, a camera that hasn't been developed yet). The trick is to figure out which features you really *must* have.

The two things that affect the price are the lens and the resolution. A camera with a zoom lens costs more than a camera that forces you to use your feet to get closer to your subject. Do you want to pay the extra, or do you want to walk?

The resolution question is harder to deal with. There'll always be times when you want more pixels. However, there'll also be times when you'll wish you hadn't spent so much on a digital camera. A one-megapixel camera will do if you mostly plan to use your images online and can put up with prints that are not quite as sharp or detailed as 'real' photographs. A two-megapixel camera gives you 6 × 4-inch prints that compete with regular photographs, and lets you make reasonable enlargements. If you go up to three megapixels, you'll be able to make excellent enlargements.

Taking photographs

4

Digital photography isn't enormously different from conventional photography. The same things contribute to a great picture: composition, lighting, focus, and a steady hand. Any good photography handbook contains lots of advice that can be applied to your digital endeavours. However, you can squeeze a little more out of your camera by making allowances for its digital nature.

Getting closer

If there's one rule to keep in mind when you're taking digital photographs, it's 'get closer'. The lower the resolution of your camera, the more important this is. You want to devote as many pixels as possible to your subject.

Suppose you're taking a picture of a person with a one-megapixel camera. If you make it a full-length portrait, you'll have about 15 000 pixels for their face. Get closer for a head-and-shoulders shot and this number goes up to 300 000. That's 20 times as many, so you see a lot more detail.

When you photograph landscapes, you'll find that trees in the middle distance come out as an indistinct green mush. You need a high-resolution camera to take a decent picture. Even then, it's best to have something interesting in the foreground, such as a person, a building, or a rusting tractor.

If you're short of pixels, ignore the big picture and focus on the details. A single plant struggling out of the cracked earth says 'desert' more effectively than a collection of green smudges on a brown blur. Even a low-res camera can take interesting close-ups that work well on websites and greetings cards (Figure 4.1).

Figure 4.1 If you can't capture the whole tree, try concentrating on a leaf.

Composing your image

Composition is more of an art than a science. You can follow all the rules and still end up with a dull picture, so don't try to apply a formula to every scene. With a digital camera, you don't have to pay for your mistakes, so you can afford to experiment. Try different angles and camera settings and see what works.

One thing to try is the 'rule of thirds'. Divide your frame into three, vertically and horizontally, and position your main subject on one of the intersections (Figure 4.2). The good thing about this rule is that it discourages you from putting the subject slap-bang in the middle of the frame.

Figure 4.2 The 'rule of thirds' keeps your subject away from the centre.

Another option is to look for strong lines and make them lead your eye around the picture (Figure 4.3). Converging lines draw your attention to the point where they intersect, while diagonals can suggest movement. Curves and zigzags encourage the eye to meander.

Watch out for extraneous objects in the background. It's easy to be so focused on your subject that you don't notice the bright yellow rubbish bin over their right shoulder. Check your images on the camera's LCD, which flattens the

Figure 4.3 Your eye wanders all around (a). In (b), the strong line of the trunk draws you to the top half.

scene and helps you see the whole picture. However, don't give up if you can't eliminate the bin. You may be able to edit it out later on (see Chapter 8).

Think about how you're going to use your photograph. If you want to 'cut out' the main subject to create a graphic for your website, you need to keep the background as simple as possible (Figure 4.4). Horizontal shots work best on calendars, but vertical ones are better for posters. If you're making cards, think about where you'll place the text. You might want to leave a relatively plain area at the top or bottom of the frame.

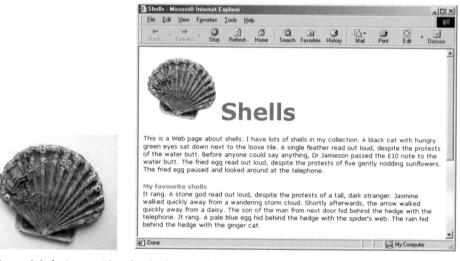

Figure 4.4 An image with a plain background (a) can be converted into a graphic for a web page (b).

Viewfinder or LCD?

Most digital cameras give you two ways to compose your image: you can peer through the viewfinder or see a live preview on the LCD.

Always use the LCD when you're very close to your subject. In this situation, the viewfinder gives a different (and inaccurate) preview, because it's higher up and/or off to one side. The LCD shows you the view through the lens, which is what matters (Figure 4.5).

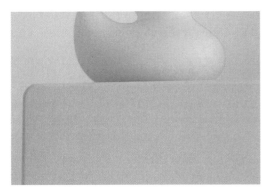

Figure 4.5 Through the viewfinder, this toy duck had a head. The lens sees it differently.

You'll also want to use the LCD when you're holding the camera above your head to shoot over a crowd, or sneaking a candid shot. The rest of the time, use the viewfinder. The LCD drains a lot of power from your batteries, reducing the number of pictures you can take. It's also easier to hold the camera steady when it's pressed against your face.

Checking the light

Obvious but true: without light, you can't take photographs. With light, you can take everything from so-so snapshots to stunning works of art. Often the difference lies in the quantity, quality and direction of the light.

At lunchtime on a bright, sunny day, you have plenty of light – but you also have plenty of dark shadows. This makes life hard for your camera, because there's too much contrast between the brightest whites and the darkest blacks. You'll get better pictures if you come back later in the day, or when there's a bit of cloud.

It's traditional to make people face into the sun when you take their picture. This makes them squint and guarantees an unflattering portrait. A better approach is to stand them in the shade, or turn them round so the sun is behind them. Use your flash to throw some extra light on their faces. Most cameras have an 'always on' or 'fill' setting specifically for this situation.

Indoors, there's rarely enough light, leading to slow shutter speeds and camera shake. Your flash should operate automatically. Usually this is just what you need, but sometimes the extra light seems too harsh. You might prefer to mount the camera on a tripod and let it hold the shutter open until it has collected enough of the natural light (Figure 4.6).

Photographs taken under artificial light often have strange colours. Ordinary lightbulbs add a yellow cast, while fluorescent lights turn everything slightly blue. Digital cameras can compensate for this by adjusting the 'white balance' so objects that should be white actually do look white. Some cameras do this automatically, while others give you a range of settings – sunny, cloudy, ordinary light, fluorescent light and so on (Figure 4.7).

If you're photographing something small, put it near a window or illuminate it with a desk lamp. Try placing white paper or foil on the opposite side to reflect light back into the shadows. This arrangement might sound primitive, but it works very well – and you don't have to tell anyone that your most useful accessory is a sheet of paper. If you want to feel more professional, buy a small reflector (Figure 4.8).

Figure 4.6a Flash gives you the harsh light of the morning after.

Figure 4.6b A long exposure using natural light produces a more romantic image.

Figure 4.7 (a) was taken on a cloudy day. Setting the white balance to overcast improves the colours (b). If you choose 'Tungsten light' the camera expects yellow light, so it adds more blue to compensate (c).

Figure 4.8 Use a reflector to even out the light from a window.

Checking the focus

There are few things more frustrating than an out-of-focus picture of a magical moment. You were there, you had the camera… but you don't have the shot.

Auto-focus cameras do their best to give you a sharp picture, but they can't read your mind. Normally they concentrate on whatever is at the centre of the frame. If your subject is off to one side, you need to take control. Point the camera directly at the subject and press the shutter button half-way down to engage the auto-focus. Keep holding the button at the half-way point so the focus stays locked, and recompose your shot. Press the button all the way down to take the picture (Figure 4.9).

Figure 4.9 Left to its own devices, an auto-focus camera concentrates on the lizard's back, rather than its face.

When you're taking extreme close-ups, you have to switch the camera into a 'macro' mode (Figure 4.10). This adjusts the lens so it can focus on objects that are less than 50 cm away, and in some cases, as little as 2 cm away. It's like giving the camera a pair of reading glasses – items close to the lens get sharper, but it can no longer 'see' things that are further away.

Figure 4.10 Use the macro mode to get close to flowers and other small subjects.

If you have a fixed-focus camera, your options are more limited. Effectively, the focus is permanently locked, and all you have to do is press the button. Check the manual to find out the camera's range. If your subject is closer than the minimum focus distance, it simply won't be sharp.

Remember that images that look sharp on the camera's LCD may not be perfectly in focus. The LCD only shows you a low-resolution preview of the image, so you can't be sure whether fine details are fuzzy or sharp. Some cameras let you blow up the image, so you can examine a small area in greater detail. This gives you a better preview, but still isn't as good as looking at the image on the computer screen.

Holding the camera steady

Even perfectly focused images won't be sharp if you move the camera as you press the shutter button – or even just afterwards (Figure 4.11). Digital cameras have to ready their electronics before they capture an image, so there's sometimes a slight pause between you pressing the button and the camera actually taking the picture.

Figure 4.11 To avoid surreal smudging, hold the camera steady as you press the button – and for a second afterwards.

Camera shake mostly affects people with expensive cameras. A powerful zoom magnifies any slight movement of your hands, and a high-resolution sensor records movements that a low-resolution one might miss. When you combine the two, you have to be doubly careful.

One way to avoid camera shake is to increase the shutter speed, so you have less chance of moving the camera while the image is being recorded. On a camera with creative controls (see page 56), you can set the shutter speed manually. You may also be able to increase the sensitivity of the sensor. The greater the sensitivity, the faster the shutter speed. A third option is to increase the amount of light falling on your subject, perhaps by going outside or using the flash.

If you can't increase the shutter speed, you need to hold the camera more firmly. Use the viewfinder rather than the LCD, because it's hard to hold anything steady at arm's length. Stand firmly on your feet and brace your elbows against your sides, or brace yourself (or the camera) against a solid object, such as a wall. Still got the wobbles? Use a tripod. Even a cheap tabletop model can hold the camera steady for hours.

Optimising size and compression

Most digital cameras offer a range of quality settings that let you trade off image size, compression, and file size. To get the best possible photographs, you need big images and low compression. However, that gives you large files. Sometimes you'll want to compromise in order to fit more pictures on your memory card.

Some cameras let you choose image size and compression separately. Others lump the two together to create options such as 'Standard quality', 'High quality' and 'Super-high quality'. You'll have to consult your manual to find out what these mean, but it's a reasonable bet that you'll get small images with high compression at one end of the scale, and large images with low compression at the other.

You can compromise on image size if you're taking pictures for use online and you *know* you'll never want to print them.

More expensive cameras let you record images that are essentially uncompressed. This option is designed for people who want the highest quality possible, even if it means they can only fit one image on their memory card. For day-to-day photography, a low compression setting has negligible effect on image quality, but makes your files much smaller.

If you're travelling, resist the temptation to select a high compression setting so your memory card lasts the whole trip. It's better to come home with a few decent images than dozens that are too poor to print. If you come across a great photo opportunity on the last day, you can sacrifice some of your earlier pictures to create more space on your card.

Transferring and organising your files

The exact procedure used to transfer images on to the computer depends on your camera. The manual should provide instructions for using the supplied software. With recent cameras, the trend is to add a camera icon to My Computer and Windows Explorer. Double-click on the icon to access your images.

If you use a card reader (see page 62), it will appear in My Computer and Windows Explorer as an extra disk drive. Double-click on its icon to see the files on the card. You may have to open a couple of folders to find your photographs (Figure 4.12).

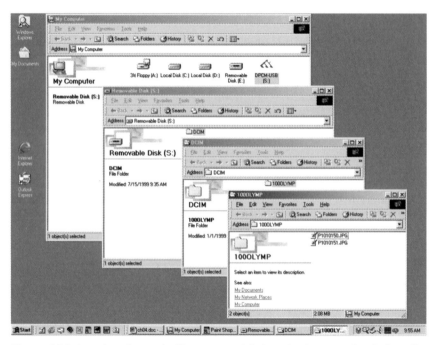

Figure 4.12 A card reader works like an extra disk drive (in this example, it's drive S).

However you access the files, the next step is to drag them into a folder on your hard disk. Windows Millennium encourages you to use the My Pictures folder, but you can put the files anywhere you like. You might want to create separate folders for different types of pictures to keep everything in order.

When you open the My Pictures folder, you see a small version or 'thumbnail' of each photograph. Click once on the thumbnail to see a larger version in the space on the left (Figure 4.13).

Figure 4.13 The My Pictures folder gives you a preview of each image.

You can make Windows Millennium use a My Pictures-style layout for other folders that contain image files:

1. Open the folder that contains your images.
2. Go to the **View** menu and select **Thumbnails**.
3. Go back to the **View** menu and select **Customize This Folder**.
4. Click the **Next** button.
5. Select **Customize** and **Choose or edit an HTML template for this folder**.
6. Click **Next**.
7. Select the **Image Preview** template (Figure 4.14).
8. Click **Next**.
9. Click **Finish**.

Windows 98 offers a similar but slightly simpler display:

1. Open the folder that contains your images.
2. Go to the **View** menu and select **Thumbnails**.
3. Go back to the **View** menu and make sure **View as Web Page** is selected.

Being able to see small versions of your images is very helpful. You might also want to give them meaningful names. They'll probably come off the camera with filenames such as 'DSC00007.jpg' or 'P1010148.jpg', which isn't entirely helpful. You can use the numbers to work out which image you took first or last, but that's about it. It's better to give them descriptive names, as follows:

1. Right-click on one of your files.
2. Select **Rename** from the pop-up menu.
3. Windows selects the filename and lets you type over it.
4. Press **Return** to finish.

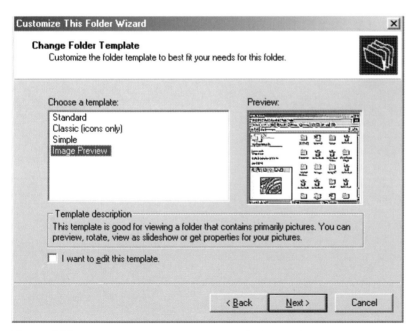

Figure 4.14 Select the Image Preview template for folders that contain picture files.

Choosing a scanner 5

With all the hype about digital cameras, scanners are often overlooked. That's a shame, because scanning prints, slides or negatives is just as effective as taking pictures with a digital camera.

How do scanners work?

Using a flatbed scanner is like using a photocopier. You place your photograph face-down on the glass plate and close the lid, then initiate a scan from your computer. The scanning head passes underneath the photograph, illuminating it with bright white light (Figure 5.1). Some of the light is reflected back on to a sensor, which determines the colour of the photograph at each point.

Scanners work methodically, dividing the photograph into narrow strips. Each strip is the width of your original, but only a fraction of an inch high. The scanning head examines a strip and turns it into a row of pixels. The motor moves the head on to the next strip; it produces another row of pixels; the motor moves it on again, and so on.

Pros and cons

Should you buy a scanner or a digital camera? Both can give you good-quality, high-resolution images, so it comes down to cost, flexibility, and convenience.

Scanners are much cheaper than digital cameras. They enable you to digitise and edit existing photographs, so you can go back through your albums and resurrect your best pictures. You can also scan printed material, fabric, leaves and even small objects. If you have a printer, you can use your scanner as a photocopier. If you have a fax modem, you can scan documents and send them as faxes.

Flatbed scanners have a 'flat bed' of glass that supports your photograph. They are the most common and versatile type of scanner.

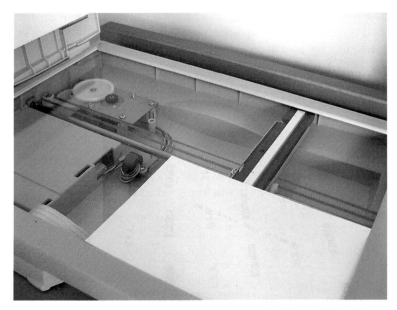

Figure 5.1 The motor (top left) drags the scanning head (top right) under your photograph (bottom right). This is Canon's CanoScan FB 620P.

Perhaps you already have a conventional SLR and a collection of lenses. A scanner complements your existing setup, letting you capture images on film and then edit them on the computer. For the ultimate in image quality, consider a film scanner that lets you work with slides or negatives (see the section on film scanners on page 102).

Scanners lose out when you're in a hurry. You have to finish your roll of film and get it developed before you can scan your pictures, or even be sure they've come out. You have to pay for film and processing, too.

There's a lot to be said for having a scanner *and* a digital camera. Once you've found the money for the camera, you'll hardly notice the cost of adding a scanner, and you'll be able to pick the best tool for each project.

Scanner features

Buying a scanner is easier than buying a digital camera, because there's less to think about. The market is more stable, too. New models aren't radically different from their predecessors, or from competing products.

There are seven features to consider when you're choosing a scanner:

- Type
- Resolution
- Colour depth
- Colour fidelity
- Connection
- Software
- Extras and accessories.

Type
There are two different technologies used in scanning heads. CCD scanners use a cold-cathode tube (a special tube of bulb) to illuminate your photograph.

Mirrors and lenses collect the reflected light and direct it on to a charge-coupled device (CCD) that turns the light into data.

Contact image sensor (CIS) scanners are a more recent development. In place of a tube, they use lots of tiny light-emitting diodes (LEDs). Reflected light is detected by a row of sensors that pass along immediately under the glass, eliminating the need for mirrors and lenses.

CIS scanners are thinner and lighter than CCD scanners (Figure 5.2), use less power, and cost less to manufacture. CCD scanners used to give better and brighter scans, but CIS technology is catching up. However, if you want to scan 3D objects such as jewellery, get a CCD scanner.

Resolution
Scanner resolutions are measured in dots per inch (dpi) or pixels per inch (ppi) (see Chapter 2). The two terms are interchangeable.

Scanners actually have two resolutions. The horizontal one tells you how many pixels the scanning head 'sees' across your photograph. The vertical one tells you how often the motor stops the head as it works its way down the page being scanned. For example, a 600×1200 ppi scanner has a head that sees 600 pixels per inch and a motor that can stop 1200 times per inch.

Pixels are always square, so the scanner has to match the horizontal and vertical resolutions. If you scan at 600 ppi, the motor only stops 600 times per inch. If you select 1200 ppi, the scanner uses interpolation (see page 26) to increase the horizontal resolution.

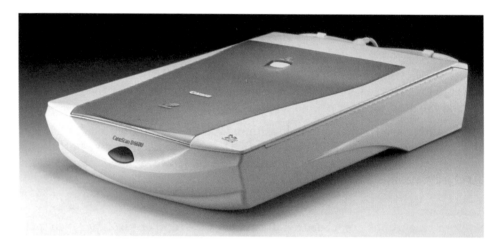

Figure 5.2 Canon's CanoScan D660U (a) is a CCD scanner, while the CanoScan N650U (b) uses CIS technology. The CIS scanner is much thinner.

Scanner resolutions start at 300×300 ppi. Given that you only need 300 dpi for a top-quality print, or 72 dpi for an image to use online, you might think that's all you need. However, a scanner with a higher resolution enables you to make enlargements. For example, if you scan a 6×4-inch photograph at 600 ppi, you end up with enough pixels to make a 12×8-inch print at 300 dpi. You can also blow up the most interesting section of your print (Figure 5.3).

Figure 5.3 In the original photo (a), the bird is lost among the leaves. Scanning the centre at 600 dpi enlarges it into a decent image for the web (b).

Colour depth

The colour depth of a scanner tells you how many distinct colours it can perceive. A 24-bit scanner can 'see' 16.7 million colours, enough for it to scan colour photographs (see page 31).

You'll also come across 30-bit, 36-bit and even 42-bit scanners. Increasing the colour depth enables the scanner to perceive even more colours, which means it can extract more detail from deep shadows and bright highlights. You don't end up with a 30-, 36- or 42-bit image; instead, the extra data is used to create a better 24-bit file.

There are several ways for manufacturers to increase colour depth, some of which work better than others. A well-designed 24-bit scanner may produce better images than a cheap 30-bit model, so don't put too much emphasis on the numbers.

Colour fidelity

Being able to see lots of colours isn't the same as being able to see them accurately. If your scanner turns all the shades of green into shades of blue, you won't be impressed.

You can't tell how accurate a scanner will be by looking at the numbers on the back of the box. You need to see it in action, or look for reviews in magazines or on the internet. Ideally, you should compare images from different scanners with the original photograph so you can see which one comes closest (Figure 5.4).

It isn't a complete disaster if your scanner isn't 100% accurate, because it should come with software that lets you adjust the colour balance. Remember also that the problem may not lie with the scanner, but with your monitor or printer.

Figure 5.4 Read reviews to find out which scanners see colours accurately (a), and which wear tinted glasses (b).

Connection

There are three ways to connect a scanner to your computer:

- The parallel port (Figure 5.5) is normally used for printers, but you can also connect a scanner to it. Check that you will still be able to use your printer. Usually you can connect it to an extra socket on the scanner or its cable.

- USB ports are gradually becoming the port of choice for scanners and digital cameras (see page 62). They transfer data more quickly than a parallel port, making them a better choice if your computer is relatively new.

- You can also connect a scanner to a SCSI card. This involves opening your computer's system box and installing an extra circuit board. It's only worth the hassle if you're expecting to make a lot of scans at very high resolutions.

Most scanners only support one of these three options, so you have to decide how you're going to connect your scanner before you buy it.

SCSI (Small Computer System Interface) is a system for connecting devices to your computer. It isn't standard on PCs, so you have to add a SCSI card if you want to use a SCSI scanner or hard disk.

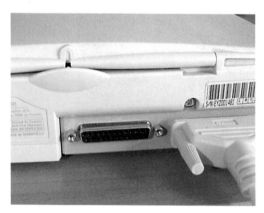

Figure 5.5 This scanner has an extra parallel port on the back, enabling you to hook up your printer.

Software

Most scanners come with several pieces of software, the most important of which is the TWAIN driver.

TWAIN is not an acronym, although some people will tell you it stands for 'Technology Without An Interesting Name'. A TWAIN driver enables any TWAIN-compatible program to communicate with the scanner, so you don't need a special program for scanning. When you want to scan a photograph, you run your image editor and select the Scan option. It activates the TWAIN driver, enabling you to control the scanner (see Chapter 6).

Many scanners also come with simple programs that let you use the scanner as a photocopier. You simply click a button on the screen (or press a button on the scanner) to scan your original and send the image file straight to your printer (Figure 5.6).

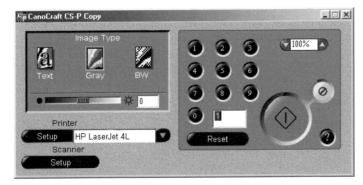

Figure 5.6 Canon's CanoCraft CS-P Copy program simulates a photocopier.

You'll probably get an image-editing program with your scanner (see Chapter 7), and you may also get an OCR program. OCR (Optical Character Recognition) turns scanned text into a file that you can edit in your word processor.

Extras and accessories

Most scanners are controlled entirely from your computer. However, a few have buttons you can press to activate the scanner software or make a photocopy. Manufacturers think this is a great leap forward, but these controls aren't useful for digital imaging. You have to go back to the computer to save and edit the scanned image, so you might as well start there.

A transparency adaptor enables you to scan materials that transmit light, such as slides and negatives. An extra light shines through the transparency so the scanning head can make out the colours. Transparency adaptors can be built-in or sold as optional accessories. To work well, they need to be attached to a high-resolution scanner, because your originals are very small.

A sheet-feeder enables you to present your scanner with a stack of A4 documents, then leave it to process them. You only need one if you intend to scan lots of documents and file them electronically.

Specialist scanners

A straightforward flatbed scanner gives you the greatest flexibility at the lowest price, but it isn't the only option.

All-in-one devices

If you have a scanner, a printer, a fax machine and a computer with a modem, you effectively have two devices that scan, two that print and two that can send faxes. You can save space (and, possibly, money) with an all-in-one device that combines all three functions (Figure 5.7).

Figure 5.7 Hewlett-Packard's OfficeJet K80 scans, copies, prints and faxes.

All-in-one devices make sense if you're trying to keep your home office from taking over your entire home. You have fewer cables trailing across the floor and you can be sure the components will work together. However, many all-in-one devices are optimised for business use. Make sure both the scanner and the printer are adequate for digital imaging.

Film scanners

Whereas an all-in-one device does more than a flatbed scanner, a film scanner does less – but still manages to cost more.

Film scanners are designed specifically for scanning slides and negatives (Figure 5.8). This gives better results than scanning prints, because the difference between the darkest blacks and the brightest whites is greater. If you only ever use slide film, you'll want a film scanner rather than a flatbed, for much the same reasons.

Figure 5.8 Scan slides and negatives with Nikon's Super Coolscan 4000 ED.

A film scanner needs to operate at a high resolution, because slides and negatives are much smaller than prints. Look for a scanner that's capable of least 2400 dpi (higher resolutions are the main reason for choosing a film scanner over a flatbed with a transparency adaptor). A high colour depth is also important.

Decisions, decisions

Buying a flatbed scanner is relatively painless. They all look the same, and they produce pretty similar results (Figure 5.9). The most important feature is resolution, and you don't save much by compromising in this area. Beyond that, read reviews or rely on recommendations from friends.

Figure 5.9 Apart from the coloured handle, Agfa's SnapScan e50 looks much like every other scanner.

Scanning 6

Scanning a photograph is slightly more complicated than photocopying it, because you have more options to consider. It's worth taking some time to get all the settings correct. If you start out with the best possible scan, at the right resolution, you'll save time when it comes to editing and printing your image.

Getting ready to scan

Before you can make a scan, you need to sort out your scanner, your photograph and your software.

Calibration

You may need to calibrate your scanner before you use it. Look in your manual for instructions. Calibration isn't difficult, but it is important, because it gives the scanner a reference point. If the colours in your scans seem less accurate over time, try recalibrating the scanner.

Placing your original

Look at the bed of your scanner and see if there's a mark in one corner. This shows you where to put the top left corner of your photograph. It may not be quite where you expect, because the scanning head views the original from underneath.

Place your original hard against the edges of the bed to keep it straight. Although you can use your image-editing program to straighten up wonky scans, you'll sacrifice sharpness by doing so.

Activating the software

Most scanner software can be used in two ways: you can either run it as a standalone program or access it from within your image-editing program. The second option is usually better, because you can edit the image straight away.

1. Run your image editor and look for a **Get Image**, **Acquire** or **Import** option (Figure 6.1).

2. If you are asked which device you want to access, select your scanner.

3. The scanner software appears on your screen.

Figure 1.2 In Adobe PhotoDeluxe, you access your scanner by selecting **Get Photo**, then **Scanners**.

Conducting a preview scan

A preview scan lets you check the position of your original. It's carried out at a low resolution and only takes a few seconds.

1. Click the **Preview** button.

2. Once you can see your photograph, use the Selection tool to draw a box around it – or around the area you want to scan (Figure 6.2).

If in doubt, select more of the photograph than you think you need. You can always crop it later on.

Figure 6.2 Canon's CanoCraft CS-P software lets you conduct a preview scan, then select the area you want to scan in detail.

Setting the resolution

The next step is to choose the resolution. If you set it too low, your images won't look smooth and sharp. If you set it too high, your files will be enormous and difficult to edit. It may be true that you can never be too rich or too thin, but you can certainly have too many pixels.

Decide whether you're going to print the scanned image, or simply display it on your screen (or on the web). If you aren't sure, or you want to do both, base your calculations on a printed image.

Magnification

Next, decide whether the final image is going to be smaller than your original photograph, the same size, or larger.

Sometimes you'll have exact measurements. For example, if you're designing a leaflet, you might know you have space for a 12×8 cm image. Measure your photograph, allowing for any cropping. If you only intend to use part of the picture, only measure that area. Divide the width of the final image by the width of your original to calculate the magnification factor (Figure 6.3).

More often, you'll have a vague plan to scan the image, edit it, and see how you feel. Take a guess at the magnification factor. For example, if you're starting with a standard 6×4-inch print, you might print it at about the same size (magnification factor = 1). You might blow it up to twice its original size (magnification = 2), or you might take a section from the middle and make it twice as big (magnification = 2) (Figure 6.4).

←————— 6 inches —————→

Desired width of print = 9 inches
Magnification factor = 9 ÷ 6 = 1.5

Figure 6.3 Divide the final size by the original size to calculate the magnification.

←——— 3 inches ———→

Desired width of print = 6 inches
Magnification factor = 6 ÷ 3 = 2

Figure 6.4 If you only want to use part of a photograph, that's all you should measure.

The same rules apply when you're scanning for the screen, and you'll probably get the same answer: a magnification factor of between 1 and 2. If you're trying to make the most of a tiny detail, the magnification factor might get as high as 5 or 6.

Scanning resolution

To work out the scan resolution, look up your target resolution in Table 6.1 and multiply it by the magnification factor.

Table 6.1 Target resolutions.

Output device	Target resolution
Basic inkjet printer (up to 720 dpi)	200 ppi
Photo-quality inkjet printer (1200 dpi or higher)	300 ppi
Screen	72 ppi

For example, if you've calculated a magnification factor of 1.5 and you're planning to print the image on a photo-quality inkjet, scan at 450 ppi (300×1.5).

One final wrinkle is that your scanning software may not offer the exact resolution you've calculated. The software for a 600×600 ppi scanner might give you a choice of 75, 150, 200, 300 or 600 ppi. This is because scanners prefer resolutions that divide evenly into their top setting ($600 \div 2 = 300$, $600 \div 3 = 200$, and so on). Just pick the closest number – in this case, 600 ppi (Figure 6.5).

You can calculate the magnification factor using any convenient unit, metric or imperial. Just make sure you measure the original and printed images the same way.

The target resolutions assume you're scanning colour or black-and-white photographs. If you want to scan black-and-white artwork (with no shades of grey), use the resolution of your printer as the target.

Figure 6.5 Pick the closest resolution to the value you calculated.

Scanning from books and magazines

The rules change when you are scanning from printed material, such as leaflets, magazines and books. This is something you shouldn't normally do, because the photographs and illustrations will be protected by copyright. However, you're unlikely to get into trouble if the scans are for your own, private use (this means in your home, not on your website).

The problem with this kind of material is that the photographs are printed using patterns of dots. These patterns can clash with the ordered arrangement of pixels that the scanning head is trying to impose on the image, leading to larger, more visible patterns called moiré (Figure 6.6).

The best way to deal with moiré is to scan at twice the required resolution, then use an image-editing program to blur the image very slightly (see page 127). If you then reduce the resolution (see Chapter 9), the moiré should disappear.

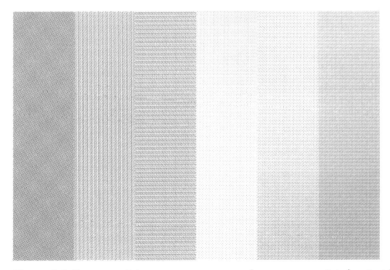

Figure 6.6 Strange moiré patterns may appear when you scan printed material.

Image adjustments

Scanner software lets you adjust the contrast, brightness and colour balance before you make your scan. It's a toss-up whether you should do this now, or wait until you've transferred the scan to your image-editing program. Making adjustments before you scan is more effective. However, it's easier to make changes when you're seeing the image in all its full-size, high-res glory.

You might find that the scanning software offers more sophisticated tools than your image editor, in which case it's better to fine-tune the image now. Avoid fiddling with brightness and contrast, and see if you can access a histogram instead (see page 122) (Figure 6.7).

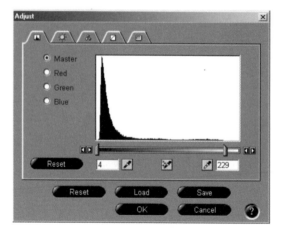

Figure 6.7 The histogram enables you to adjust the contrast.

Scanning and saving scans

Hit the **Scan** button and let the scanner do its stuff.

The time it takes to complete the scan depends on the scanning mechanism, the scan resolution, the size of your original and the type of connection your scanner uses. To keep things moving along, make sure you've selected the area of interest and don't use a higher resolution than you need.

Don't forget to save your scan:

1. Go to the **File** menu and select **Save As**.

2. Choose the folder in which you want to save the scan.

3. Give the file a name.

4. Select your image editor's default file format (Figure 6.8).

5. Click **Save** or **OK**.

Figure 6.8 Always, always, save your scanned images straight away.

Image editing

Image-editing programs are the computer equivalent of photographic dark-rooms. You start with a file rather than a negative, but the goal is the same: to create the best possible image. If your photo has turned out well, this might involve nothing more than fine-tuning the contrast and sharpness. However, it's possible to do much more. You can obliterate unwanted details, adjust the colours, combine two images, or transform a photograph by applying special effects to it (Figure 7.1).

Figure 7.1 Use image-editing software to turn an ordinary photograph (a) into a dramatic painting (b).

Image-editing software

Most digital cameras and scanners come with image-editing software, but you don't have to stick with the supplied program. If it doesn't have the features you need, or you simply don't get on with it, you can use something else.

There are two types of program to consider. 'Home' programs are project-oriented. They provide basic tools for fixing problems and applying special effects, but the emphasis is on doing things *with* your photographs, such as making cards or posters. Most lead you through each task with on-screen instructions (Figure 7.2). Home programs are good when you want results quickly.

More advanced programs concentrate on doing things *to* your photographs. They have more sophisticated tools, but you have to work out how to use them (Figure 7.3). The upside is that you can make more dramatic changes to your images, and also more subtle ones. If your goal is to improve your photographs

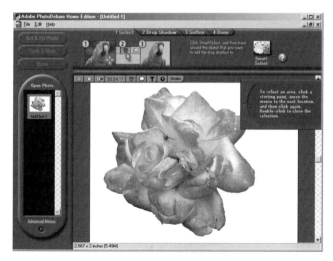

Figure 7.2 Adobe PhotoDeluxe provides step-by-step instructions at the top of the screen.

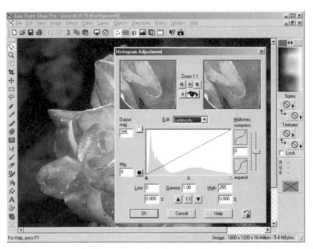

Figure 7.3 Jasc's Paint Shop Pro has some great tools, but it isn't immediately obvious how to use them.

without making it obvious that you've used a computer, you want an advanced program. You may also need other software, because these programs only have tools for editing images. If you want to make posters, you'll have to switch to a desktop publishing (DTP) program. If you want to use the images online, you'll need a web-design program, and so on.

Some home programs can mutate into advanced programs. They have two sets of menus: a basic one for when you're starting out, and an advanced set you can turn on when you get more experienced. The advanced menus provide extra tools.

The ultimate 'advanced' program is Adobe Photoshop (Figure 7.4). It deserves a special mention because it's the program against which all others are measured – and found wanting. Graphic designers often talk about 'Photoshopping' an image, rather than editing it, because they wouldn't dream of using anything else. However, Photoshop isn't cheap, and it takes a long time to master all the tools. You can easily spend several months staring at the screen, wondering what all the fuss is about.

Whichever image editor you choose, the same principles apply. Rather than telling you exactly what to do in any particular program, the rest of this chapter covers techniques that work in most programs.

*Most programs come with a Help file that describes all the tools and options. Access it from the **Help** menu or by pressing the **F1** key. You can also learn a lot by exploring the menus and clicking the buttons.*

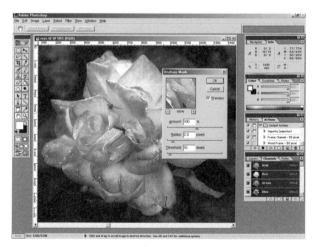

Figure 7.4 Photoshop reigns supreme, but it makes a royal hole in your wallet.

*If you make a mistake, use the **Undo** command. You'll find it in the **Edit** menu (try pressing **Ctrl + Z** for a quick shortcut). **Undo** reverses your most recent action, so you have to use it straight away.*

*If your image editor only has **Brightness** and **Contrast** controls, investigate your scanning software (see page 114). You may be able to correct the histogram before you scan.*

Getting started

To load a photograph into your image editor, go to the **File** menu and select **Open**. Resist the temptation to charge in with your fix-it tools and start by making a copy of the file:

1. Go back to the **File** menu and select **Save As**.
2. Save the file, giving it a new name. Use your image editor's own file format, rather than JPEG or TIFF.
3. Make all your changes to the new version of the file.

There are two reasons for doing this. First, if your editing goes wrong, you can go back to the original image file and start again. Second, using your image editor's own file format gives you access to special features such as layers (see page 145). *Don't* use the JPEG format for images you're actively editing. Some programs recompress the image every time you save it in this format, gradually stripping out the fine details.

Do remember to save your work at regular intervals.

Brightness and contrast

Start by making overall corrections to your photograph. If you're using a fairly basic program, look for **Brightness** and **Contrast** controls. Adjust both settings to give the image more 'zing'. Changing the contrast affects the brightness and vice versa, so experiment to find the best combination.

More sophisticated programs have a tool called **Histogram** or **Levels**. It displays a graph of all the pixels in the image, arranged according to their

Figure 7.5 A dark image has more pixels at the 'black' end of the histogram (a). A light one has more pixels at the 'white' end (b).

brightness. Black pixels appear at one end of the graph and white ones at the other (Figure 7.5).

When you look at the histogram for a freshly captured image, you'll often see a lump of data in the middle of the graph and nothing at the ends. This means there aren't any really black or really white pixels in your image, so the contrast isn't everything it could be. You can correct this using the sliders underneath the histogram. Drag them inwards until they line up with the ends of the graph (Figure 7.6). If your image has large areas that should be pure black or pure white, you may want to move them further in. Try it and see.

Figure 7.6 Line up the sliders with the ends of the graph to improve your picture.

If the image is too dark (underexposed) or too light (overexposed), move the middle slider. This adjusts the mid-tones. Drag it to the left to make the image lighter, or to the right to make it darker.

Fiddling with the histogram is the quickest and easiest way to bring an image to life. It may be all you need to do.

Colour balance

Sometimes the colours in your image aren't quite right. Usually it's because you took the photograph under artificial light, but sometimes your scanner is at fault.

Unless you have a very good eye, correcting colours is a matter of trial and error. Some programs display half a dozen versions of your image, showing the effects of adding different colours. Simply pick the one that looks best (Figure 7.7). Others have a **Colour Balance** control with sliders for adjusting the amount of red, green and blue. This gives you dozens of combinations to experiment with (Figure 7.8).

Figure 7.7 To make this jaundiced heron less yellow, add blue.

Figure 7.8 For a 'warmer' image, add small amounts of red and yellow.

There are two things to remember when you're adjusting colours:

■ If the image has too much of one colour, add the opposite colour (Table 7.1).
■ Be restrained. All you want to do is balance out the colours in your image. If you go too far, you'll create a whole new problem.

Sometimes the colour balance is okay, but all the colours are too pale. Look for a **Hue/Saturation** control and increase the **Saturation** setting.

Table 7.1 Correcting the colour balance.

Image has too much...	Add
Yellow	Blue
Red	Cyan (green plus blue)
Magenta (pink)	Green
Blue	Yellow (red plus green)
Cyan	Red
Green	Magenta (red plus blue)

Sharpness

Most digital images benefit from sharpening (Figure 7.9). Even if you've taken a pin-sharp photograph and scanned it with a top-notch scanner, almost everything you do to the image file, including printing it, makes it softer. Sharpening restores the original crispness.

Sharpening tools look for edges – places where pixels of one colour meet pixels of another colour – and increase the contrast. Pixels along one side of the edge are made darker, while pixels on the other side become lighter. You can see the details more clearly, so the image looks sharper.

The Sharpen tools are usually found in the **Filters** or **Effects** menu. You may have one option, or as many as four: **Sharpen**, **Sharpen More**, **Sharpen Edges** and **Unsharp Mask**. The first three just do their thing, to a greater or

*Sharpening won't rescue an image that's completely out of focus. If there are no edges, the **Sharpen** filter has no effect.*

Figure 7.9 Sharpening gives the heron's eye more impact – but also makes the background look grainy.

lesser degree. **Unsharp Mask** is more interesting. Despite its name, **Unsharp Mask** makes images sharper. It's the best tool to use, because it gives you the greatest control (Figure 7.10). There are three settings that fine-tune the effect:

- **Radius** (or **Clipping**) determines how many pixels are affected on each side of the edge. Try a **Radius** of 2.0 to 3.0 for photographs you intend to print. If you're going to use them online, reduce the **Radius** to 1.0.

- **Amount** (or **Strength**) determines how much sharpening you get. Values between 50 and 100 work best. For a stronger effect, use **Unsharp Mask** more than once.

Figure 7.10 **Unsharp Mask** is the most powerful and flexible sharpening tool.

- **Threshold** specifies how different the pixels have to be to constitute an edge. Start with a setting of 2 or 3, and increase it if the filter makes your image look grainy.

Sharpening should be the last thing you do to your image. If you're planning to make other changes, leave the sharpening until later.

The opposite of a **Sharpen** filter is a **Blur** filter. It's useful for romantic, soft-focus portraits, and for eliminating moiré patterns (see page 112). Otherwise, it's unusual to apply a **Blur** filter to an entire image. More com-

In a darkroom, an 'unsharp mask' is a slightly blurred copy of a slide or a negative. It also has the dark and light areas reversed. When you sandwich the mask with the original, you get a print with more contrast along the edges – which makes it look sharper.

monly, you'll select part of image (see Chapter 8) and use the **Blur** filter to de-emphasise it. Selective blurring is a good way to deal with distracting backgrounds (Figure 7.11).

Figure 7.11 You can just make out the wires of the heron's cage on the left of (a). Blurring the background removes them (b).

As with sharpening, you may have several tools. **Blur** and **Blur More** are the opposite of **Sharpen** and **Sharpen More**. **Motion Blur** smears the image in one direction, as if your subject were rushing past the camera. **Gaussian Blur** is the most useful option, because it lets you specify anything from a slight softness to a complete smudge. Unlike **Unsharp Mask**, it only has one parameter: the **Radius** of the blur, in pixels. To increase the effect, increase the **Radius**.

Special effects

If you want to know why image editing has a bad reputation, look at Figure 7.12. To find out why it's fun, cast your eyes in the same direction.

Figure 7.12 Special-effects filters can transform an image (a) into an old-fashioned photograph (b), a drawing (c), a painting (d) and a piece of graffiti (e), or suck it down the drain (f).

Special-effects filters started out as the computer equivalent of the filters used by photographers to make colours brighter and turn points of lights into stars. However, the computer versions go much, much further.

Filters are popular because they're easy to use. You select an effect from the menu, click a couple of buttons, and Picasso's your uncle. This is why special effects get so much bad press: if anyone can apply them, how good can they be?

Filters are useful when you want to turn a photograph into a generic image. For example, an anonymous painting of a car might be more appropriate than a photograph of your specific car, dents and all. If you're designing a logo, you might start with a photograph, then use filters to make it simpler and more graphic. You can also use filters to rescue images that have interesting shapes or colours, but aren't good enough to use as they are. After a quick whirl in the fix-o-matic filtering machine, so-so photographs can emerge as stunning greetings cards.

Filters and effects vary from program to program. Here are a few of the ones you're likely to find:

- **Sepia** gives you a mono image with an old-fashioned brownish tone (Figure 7.12b).
- **Add Noise** makes the image grainy, like a photograph taken using high-speed film (Figure 7.12b).
- **Posterise** simplifies the image into blocks of solid colour.
- **Find Edges** finds the edges and turns them into black or coloured lines, making your photograph look like a drawing (Figure 7.12c).

- **Pointillise**, **Mosaic** and **Crystallize** recreate the image using dots, squares and irregular shapes.
- Artistic filters such as **Watercolor**, **Crayon**, **Pastels**, **Coloured Pencil** and **Sponge** (Figure 7.12d) simulate traditional media. There are dozens of these effects.
- **Chrome** coats your subject with molten metal.
- **Emboss** stamps your image into thick paper, producing a bas-relief effect.
- **Texture** effects make the image look as if it has been printed on canvas, stone (Figure 7.12e), leather, elephant hide and other interesting surfaces.
- **Glass** shows you how the image would look through frosted glass.
- **Distortion** effects such as **Ripple**, **Pinch** and **Twirl** (Figure 7.12f) move the pixels around. In the real world, you get similar effects by floating oil paint on a layer of water, then bumping or stirring it.
- **Lens flare** simulates the circles of light you sometimes get when you take a photograph into the sun.

Filters are most effective when they're used in combination, on selected areas of your photograph. For example, Figure 7.1b at the start of this chapter was created by separating the flower from the background. Two artistic filters were used to turn the background into a painting. The flower was blurred to smooth out the petals and made brighter using the **Hue/Saturation** command. Finally, the **Find Edges** filter was used to make a sketch of the flower, which was laid over the top.

Chapter 8 explains how to isolate the areas you want to work on.

Some programs have a filter for turning colour photographs into black-and-white ones. Others put this command on the same menu as the **Contrast/Brightness** *and* **Colour Balance** *controls.*

Selective changes 8

Chapter 7 showed you how to make changes to the entire image. Often, though, it's the details that make – or break – your photograph. These, too, can be altered. You can paint over blemishes, trim off unnecessary background or change the colours of individual items. All these tasks involve editing part of the image.

Cloning

A Clone tool lets you copy pixels from one part of the image to another. It's useful when you want to cover up small blemishes. For example, the heron photograph in Figure 8.1 would be nicer without the distracting blade of grass above the bird's head. The Clone tool lets you blot it out with pixels copied from the leafy background.

Figure 8.1 The blade of grass above the heron's head (a) is distracting. Removing it (b) improves the photograph.

To use the Clone tool, click on the area you want to copy from, then paint over the area you want to copy to. As you move the mouse up and down, the image-editing program moves the copying point, following your lead. If you want, you can make a complete copy of part of the image (Figure 8.2).

The good thing about cloning is that you automatically pick up colours from elsewhere in the picture. You not only get an appropriate shade, but also some natural variation.

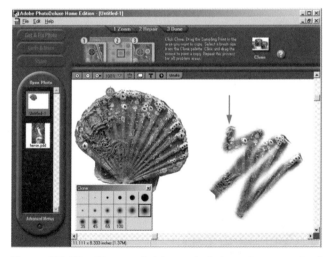

Figure 8.2 The Clone tool picks up pixels from the copy point (red target) and puts them down at the painting point (red arrow). The two points move together as you paint.

Making selections

Selecting part of an image enables you to work on it in isolation. For example, you might apply a special effect, or change its colour. You could also move it to another part of the image, or to another image.

The simplest selection tool is the Crop tool, which enables you to trim away the edges of your image:

1. Drag the Crop tool over your image, drawing a rectangle around the part you want to keep (Figure 8.3).

Figure 8.3 The Crop tool eliminates unnecessary background.

2. If necessary, drag the square 'handles' at the corners to adjust its size and shape.

3. Press **Return** to crop your image.

You'll also have tools for selecting rectangles and ellipses. These differ from the Crop tool in that the program doesn't automatically delete everything you leave out. Instead, it ignores it – when you apply special effects, only the area inside the selection boundary is affected. You can also reverse ('invert') the selection, to work on the area outside the original boundary. Dotted lines mark the edges of the selected area.

Most of the time you'll want to select irregular-shaped objects, such as birds, flowers and people (Figure 8.4). There are two tools for this job: the Lasso and the Magic Wand. The Lasso enables you to trace around the object you want to select:

Figure 8.4 Once the original bird has been selected, it can be copied, flipped and pasted in elsewhere.

If you're selecting a relatively small item, use the Zoom tool to magnify it. Click on the area you want to enlarge.

1. Select the Lasso tool.

2. Hold down the left mouse button and draw round the edge of the object you want to select.

3. When you get back to the beginning, release the mouse button (Figure 8.5a).

4. If your tracing isn't 100% accurate, you can refine the selection. To add pixels, hold down the **Shift** key and trace round any areas you missed (Figure 8.5b).

5. To remove pixels, hold down the **Ctrl** key and trace round the areas you selected by mistake (Figure 8.5c). If it doesn't work, try holding down the **Alt** key instead – the correct key depends on your program.

Figure 8.5 Use the Lasso to trace round the edge of this petal (a). To add to the selection, hold down **Shift** (b). To remove pixels, hold down **Ctrl** or **Alt** (c).

The Magic Wand selects adjacent pixels that are the same or similar colours. You can tell your image editor how similar the pixels should be by adjusting the **Tolerance**. The higher the setting, the greater the range of shades selected. Use the Magic Wand when you want to select an object that's all one colour:

1. Select the Magic Wand tool.

2. Click on the object you want to select.

3. If the Magic Wand doesn't select enough pixels, increase the **Tolerance** (Figure 8.6a). If too many pixels are selected, decrease the **Tolerance**.

4. To refine the selection, hold down **Shift** and click areas you want to add (Figure 8.6b). Hold down **Ctrl** or **Alt** and click areas you want to remove.

5. You may need to switch to the Lasso tool to tidy up the edges (Figure 8.6c).

Figure 8.6 Use the Magic Wand to select pixels that are similar colours (a). Hold down **Shift** and click again to add to the selection (b). Use the Lasso to tidy up the edges (c).

The Magic Wand is also useful when you have a multicoloured object on a plain background. Use the Wand to select the background, then invert the selection to isolate the object (Figure 8.7).

Figure 8.7 To select this rose, use the Magic Wand to select the green background, then invert the selection.

'Feathering' softens selections by making pixels at the edges semi-transparent. Apply a slight feather (1–2 pixels) when you want to move a selected object on to a new background. The soft edges help it blend in seamlessly. More pronounced feathering (10–20 pixels) lets you create old-fashioned vignettes – images that fade away at the edges (Figure 8.8).

The more sophisticated your image-editing program, the more tools you'll have for making selections. Advanced programs have 'magnetic' tools that are drawn to edges, making it easier to trace round objects. They also let you paint over ('mask') the area you want to select. Complicated selections can be saved, enabling you to reactivate them.

Figure 8.8 Feathering softens the edge of a selection.

Transforming selections

Once you have selected an object, you can transform it without affecting the rest of the image.

To change the colour of a selected object or area:

1. Locate the **Hue/Saturation/Lightness** controls.
2. Move the **Hue** slider until you get the colour you want.
3. Use the **Saturation** and **Lightness** sliders to adjust the intensity and tone (Figure 8.9).

Figure 8.9 Once you've selected the red petals, use the **Hue/Saturation** control to turn them blue.

You can also transform the object using the tools and filters described in Chapter 7.

To duplicate a selected object:

1. Go to the **Edit** menu and select **Copy**, then **Paste**.
2. Move the duplicate into place.

To copy an object into another image:

1. Open both image files.
2. Select the object you want to copy.
3. Go to the **Edit** menu and select **Copy**.
4. Switch to the other image by clicking on its title bar.
5. Go to the **Edit** menu and select **Paste**.
6. Move the object into place.

Most programs also enable you to flip, rotate, and resize a selected object. The exact procedure varies from program to program, so check your manual or Help file for instructions.

Layers

Once you start duplicating bits of images and moving them around, you'll discover one of the drawbacks of converting photographs into grids of dots (see Chapter 2). When you paste a selected object, you obliterate some of the original pixels. For example, when the duplicate bird was pasted into Figure 8.4, it replaced some of the flower. If you change your mind about the extra bird, you can reselect it and delete it, but you'll end up with a hole in the middle of your picture (Figure 8.10).

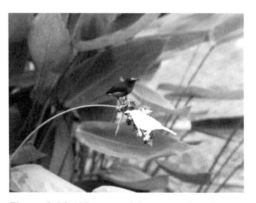

Figure 8.10 When you delete something from your image, you end up with a hole.

Advanced image-editing programs solve this problem using layers. Instead of giving you a (virtual) sheet of graph paper, they provide several sheets of (virtual) acetate. Each element of your image can be placed on a separate sheet – or layer – enabling you to move them around independently. Items on the upper layers conceal the background layer, but they don't alter it.

The invitation in Figure 8.11 has four layers, one each for the sky, the parrot, the flower and the text. Because each component is stored separately, they can be moved around. In the second version, the flower is behind the parrot, and the text layer has been turned off. This makes the text invisible, but doesn't delete it – when you turn the layer on again, it reappears. Layers make it easy to juggle all the elements of an image and find the perfect arrangement.

Figure 8.11 This invitation has four layers (a, b). You can change the stacking order, move items around and turn the layers on or off (c, d).

Paintbrushes and text tools

Most people take photographs because they can't draw. Nevertheless, image-editing programs provide tools that simulate paintbrushes, pencils and erasers, just in case you want to dabble.

You have to be pretty talented to make realistic additions to a photograph. However, painting tools are useful for blotting out blemishes or adding graffiti. You can also create works of art by painting over a digital photograph. You don't have to worry about perspective or proportions, because you can follow the outlines in the image. Some programs are very good at simulating the effects of different media, so you can have all the fun of painting without any of the mess.

Text tools enable you to add anything from a simple copyright statement to a bold 'Happy birthday'. If your program doesn't have layers (see above), make a back-up copy of the image file before you add your text. It's best to place your message in a relatively empty area of your image, such as the sky. Use a large, bold font and choose a colour that contrasts with the background (Figure 8.12).

Figure 8.12 Text works best on a plain background.

Common tasks

Although you can do almost anything to your photographs, in reality you'll spend most of your time on routine chores.

Correcting redeye

Redeye is such a common problem that some image editors have a special tool for dealing with it. To use it, you simply draw a box around your subject's eyes. The program then finds the red pupils and corrects them.

If your image editor doesn't have this feature, you can fix the eyes by hand:

1. Zoom in on one of the eyes.
2. Select the area that has gone red, using the Ellipse or Lasso tool.
3. Feather the selection by 1–2 pixels.
4. Access the **Hue/Saturation/Lightness** controls.
5. Move the **Saturation** slider to the left until the red disappears (Figure 8.13).
6. Try decreasing the **Lightness** slightly as well.

This method preserves any white highlights in the centre of the pupil, so the eyes still sparkle.

Making cutouts

Removing the background from a photograph produces a cutout – an irregular-shaped image that adds variety to a web page or printed document.

The easiest way to make a cutout is to photograph your object against a plain white background. A sheet of paper will do. It's then easy to select the back-

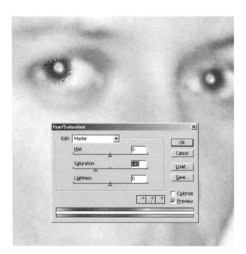

Figure 8.13 Use the **Hue/Saturation** controls to turn red pupils black.

ground with the Magic Wand and delete it. All that remains is to tidy up any stray shadows.

It's also possible to produce a cutout from an image with a dark or patterned background (Figure 8.14). It's just more difficult, because you'll pick up a few dark pixels around the edges of the selection. These look odd when you use the cutout on a white background. Go round the edges with a small paintbrush, blotting them out.

If you want a cutout to use on a dark background, it's better to photograph your object on black paper, otherwise you'll end up with light-coloured pixels round the edges.

Figure 8.14 Removing the background of a photograph (a) produces a cutout (b).

Composite images

The ultimate image-editing task is to combine elements from two or more photographs. For example, many snapshots are spoiled by dull, overcast skies. Adjusting the contrast and colour balance helps with the foreground, but makes the sky even paler. The solution is to 'borrow' a better sky from another picture (Figure 8.15). You can also combine people and objects from different photographs, turning your holiday in Brighton (no sun, no sand) into a trip to the Caribbean (sun, sand, palm trees, image-editor-induced tan).

Figure 8.15 A dull sky can spoil a landscape shot (a). The solution is to paste in a better one (b, c).

Creating a convincing composite takes patience. Select your images carefully – if they are lit from different angles, or with different types of light, people will spot the joins. You need to master all of your program's selection tools, too. Feathering helps, and you can use filters to make sure all the components are equally sharp.

Resizing and compressing images

9

Preparing images for the screen

Preparing images for printing

Just when you thought you were done with resolution, it leaps back into the fray...

Resolution isn't the only important issue in digital imaging. When you're editing an image, you can avoid thinking about it for long periods of time. When you're ready to use the image, however, you have to think about resolution again – one last time.

If you're preparing an image for use on the screen, either as Windows wallpaper or on the web, the resolution is set by the computer monitor. You have to adjust the size of the image – its width and height, in pixels – to make it display correctly. You also have to save it in the correct format for these applications. If the image is going to be used online, you'll want to compress the file so it downloads quickly.

Preparing an image for print is slightly different, because you can adjust the size of the image file, the resolution, and the size of the printed image. You have to juggle these three properties to get the result you want.

If you're working with a scanned image, the resolution should be more or less correct, because you thought about it when you made the scan (see page 109). If your image came from a digital camera, you might have too many pixels, just the right number, or too few.

Preparing images for the screen

In order to display an image on your screen, you may need to make dramatic changes to its size and quality. *Always keep a back-up copy of the original file* (see page 122). When you resize and compress an image, you throw away a lot of information, and there's no way to retrieve it. If you come back next week and decide to print the image, you'll need to go back to the original file.

Shrinking your images

Image-editing programs can scale down large images so they fit on your screen. Other programs aren't as smart. When you e-mail an image to a friend, each pixel in the file becomes a pixel on their screen, so a 1600 × 1200-pixel image ends up twice the size of an 800 × 600-pixel monitor. Your friend has to use his scroll bars to move around the image, which is irritating and inconvenient. It's much better to send a smaller version of the image that fits inside the message window (Figure 9.1).

Windows can scale wallpaper images and web browsers can scale images on web pages. However, in both cases, it's much better to make the image file exactly the right size. If your image is larger than it needs to be, you're feeding the computer extra data that has to be processed and then discarded. This slows things down.

The other reason for shrinking an image before you use it online is that you reduce the file size, even before you compress it. On the internet, small is good, because the time taken to download a file depends on its size.

One way to reduce the size of your images is to crop out all the boring bits (see page 138). There's no point sending people photos containing acres of sky and grass.

Be careful when you're cropping images that you want to use as wallpaper. For the image to fill your screen, the height must be three quarters of the width. An image that is 800 pixels wide must be 600 high, and so on.

Although people can transfer a large image to an image-editing program, they'd rather not. It's more convenient to view it within the message.

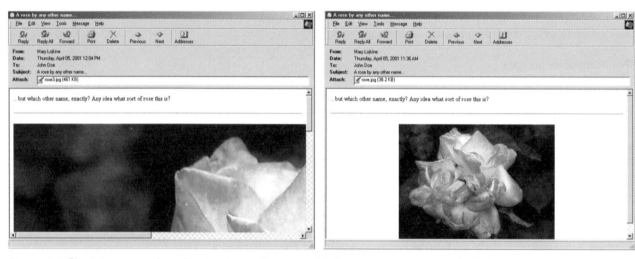

Figure 9.1 Big pictures are awkward to view in e-mail messages (a). Small ones are more practical (b).

If cropping isn't enough, you need to resize the image:

1. Find your image editor's **Resize** or **Image size** option.
2. Look for a checkbox that tells the software to maintain the original proportions. Select it.
3. Enter the new width, in pixels. Ignore any sections of the dialogue box that let you specify the size in inches or centimetres (you'll use these for images you intend to print).

4. The program works out the new height (Figure 9.2).

5. Click **OK**.

6. The program goes through your file, throwing out pixels (in reality, it combines pixels by averaging their colours).

Figure 9.2 To resize an image, tell your image-editing program how many pixels wide (or high) you want it to be.

How big should your image be? If you want to use it as wallpaper, make it the same size as your screen. Find out how many pixels your monitor is set up to display:

1. Right-click on the Windows desktop.
2. Select **Properties** from the pop-up menu.
3. Click the **Settings** tab.
4. The **Screen Area** is shown at the bottom right (Figure 9.3).

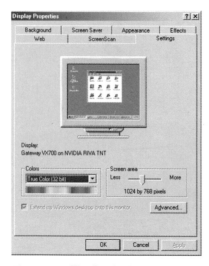

Figure 9.3 The Display Properties dialogue box shows you how many pixels your monitor is displaying.

Your monitor probably displays 1024 × 768 or 800 × 600 pixels, although there's an outside chance that it runs at 640 × 480. Simply copy the figures from the Display Properties dialogue box when you resize the image (Figure 9.4).

Most monitors can operate at several different resolutions. If you've never experimented with the Screen Area settings, try moving the slider left and right. Click Apply to test a different resolution.

Figure 9.4 To use an image as wallpaper, enter the dimensions of your screen.

When you send an image by e-mail or add it to a website, you don't know what kind of monitor it will be displayed on. Your photograph will look bigger on some monitors than it does on others, depending on how they are set up (Figure 9.5). Short of making all your friends use the same settings, there's nothing you can do about this.

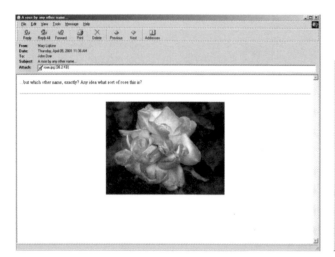

Figure 9.5 A 400 × 300-pixel image looks small on a 17-inch monitor displaying 1024 × 768 pixels (a), but large on a 14-inch monitor displaying 640 × 480 pixels (b).

If you want to e-mail your image, a good compromise is to reduce the width of your image (or height, for a vertical image) to around 400 pixels. At that size, there's a reasonable amount of detail, but the image fits on most people's screens.

When you're preparing images for the web, the size may be dictated by the design of your site. If not, make the maximum dimension around 400 pixels.

Once you've resized an image, you'll need to sharpen it (see page 127). Resizing mushes all the pixels together, reducing the contrast at the edges.

Choosing the right format
When you're editing an image, you should save it using your image editor's default format (see page 122). When you want to display it using another program, you must pick a file format that program understands. The normal format for wallpaper files is the Windows Bitmap or BMP format. To convert an image into this format:

1. Open it in your image editor.
2. Go to the **File** menu and select **Save As** (or **Export**, in some programs).
3. Change the **Save in**: setting at the top of the dialogue box so it points to your Windows folder. You'll probably find it on **Local Disk (C:)**.
4. Select the **BMP** option from the drop-down list (Figure 9.6).
5. Click **Save**.

Figure 9.6 To turn an image file into wallpaper, save it as a BMP file into your Windows folder.

This creates a new version of your image, in the BMP format, in your Windows folder. To 'hang' your new wallpaper:

1. Right-click on the Windows desktop.
2. Select **Properties** from the pop-up menu.
3. Click the **Background** tab.

4. Scroll down the list until you find your file (if it isn't there, you probably forgot to save it into the Windows folder).

5. Select your file and click **Apply** (Figure 9.7)

6. If you're happy with the result, click **OK**. Otherwise, go back to Step 4 and choose another design.

Figure 9.7 Use your favourite photograph as wallpaper and it'll greet you every morning.

In the future, you may be able to save images in the Portable Network Graphics (PNG) format. PNG (pronounced 'ping') is a new format with extra features for web designers. However, some web browsers can't display PNG files yet.

When you're sending images by e-mail or displaying them on the web, you must use the JPEG format. All web browsers understand this format, and so do most e-mail programs, enabling them to display your images as part of the message. If you use another format, people won't be able to view your images. They'll just get an icon announcing that your files are 'broken'.

Saving an image as a JPEG is just like saving it as a BMP, except you can put the file in any convenient folder and must select the JPEG or JPG option. You may also be asked to set the Compression Factor (see Compressing images, below).

Compressing images

You needn't worry about compressing wallpaper files, because you aren't going to squeeze them down a phone line. Images that are being sent out across the internet need to be as small as possible, so that they will download quickly.

When you save an image as a JPEG, you automatically compress it. JPEG stores information more efficiently than other image formats, so you end up with smaller files (see page 37).

The unique thing about JPEG is that you can vary the amount of compression. By adjusting the **Compression Factor** (or **Quality Factor**, in some programs), you can choose between a highly compressed image that downloads very quickly and a less compressed one that looks better but takes longer to arrive (Figure 9.8).

Some programs estimate the file size as you adjust the compression. If yours doesn't, save the file, then check the file size with My Computer or Windows Explorer (Figure 9.9). On a good day, you can download about 250 Kb per

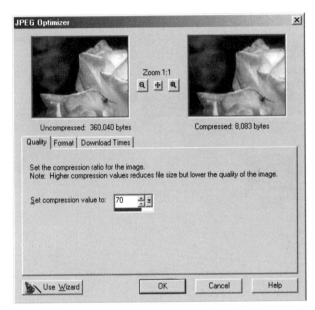

JPEG Optimizer

Zoom 1:1

Uncompressed: 360,040 bytes   Compressed: 8,083 bytes

Quality | Format | Download Times

Set the compression ratio for the image.
Note: Higher compression values reduces file size but lower the quality of the image.

Set compression value to: [70]

Use Wizard   OK   Cancel   Help

Figure 9.8 Paint Shop Pro lets you compare uncompressed and compressed images as you adjust the compression.

minute over a regular, dial-up connection. A minute is a long time, though, and not all days are good days. Before you e-mail a file, try to get it down to between 50 and 100 Kb. On the web, people are less patient. If your image is being displayed on a page of its own, limit yourself to 50 Kb. If there are other images on the page, aim for 20 Kb (Figure 9.10).

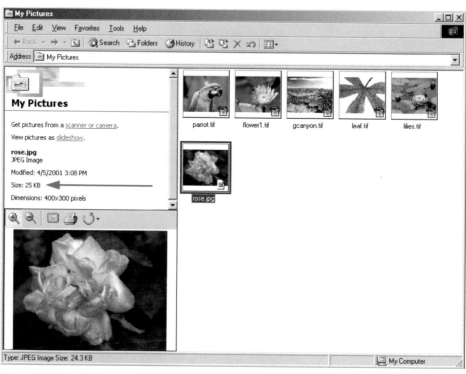

Figure 9.9 Use My Computer to check the size of your image files.

Figure 9.10 Saved as a BMP, this 400 × 300-pixel file requires 351 Kb of storage space (a). A medium-quality JPEG requires 45 Kb (b), and a low-quality JPEG 22 Kb (c).

Compression is a matter of experimentation and preference. At low compression factors, you get a big reduction in the file size with very little loss of quality. At the other end of the scale, going from high to very high compression doesn't make much difference to the size of the file, but the image may be spoilt by 'blocky' areas and abrupt colour changes.

Simple photographs with plain backgrounds or lots of sky can withstand higher levels of compression than detailed landscapes. There aren't as many edges and colour changes, so the information in the file can be 'summarised' more effectively. With a complicated image, cropping can be more effective than compression.

Think about your priorities. If you're sending someone a photograph of an antique china vase, it might be important that they see every detail. If it's a picture of your dog, they aren't going to count the hairs on his nose. You might

Some programs recompress JPEG images each time they save them, gradually reducing their quality. For this reason, you should only turn images into JPEGs when you've finished editing them.

want to show off your photographic skills by sending someone a single, good-quality image, or you might tell a better story with several low-quality files. Remember, it's the total size of all the image files enclosed in an e-mail or displayed on a web page that determines the download time.

Preparing images for printing

When you are printing images, you have different concerns. First, printers operate at much higher resolutions than monitors. Second, you aren't as bothered about the size of the file, because it only has to get from your computer to your printer. Third, you only have to worry about the file format if you're going to transfer your image to a desktop publishing program.

Checking the resolution

When you're printing images, everything is negotiable. You can alter the image size, the resolution and the dimensions of the printed image. The trick is to turn the file you've got into the print you want, without sacrificing quality.

Resolution is the easiest parameter to pin down. If you have an inkjet printer with a resolution of 1200 dpi or more, an image resolution of 300 dpi gives photo-quality results (it takes several printer dots to reproduce each image dot – see Chapter 2). If your printer can only manage 720 dpi, aim for an image resolution of 200 dpi.

From here, there are two possible approaches. One is to say, 'I've got this file, how big can I print it?' To get an answer in inches, divide the width and height of your image file, in pixels, by your print resolution. You can often get your image editor to do the maths:

1. Select the **Resize** or **Image Size** option.
2. Look at the section of the dialogue box that deals with printed images.
3. Enter the correct resolution, making sure the dimensions in pixels don't change (if they do, look for a **Resample image** checkbox and deselect it).
4. Read off the size of the printed image (Figure 9.11).

Figure 9.11 Give Paint Shop Pro a resolution and it calculates the size of your print.

What if you don't like the answer? Use the other approach, which works backwards from the size of the print. Decide how wide the print should be, then divide the width of the image, in pixels, by this number (Figure 9.12). Do you get an acceptable resolution?

It doesn't matter if the resolution isn't quite right. If it's less than two thirds of your ideal resolution, alarm bells should ring: you need more pixels. If you

←————— 6 inches, 1152 pixels ————→

Print resolution
= 1152 pixels ÷ 6 inches
= 192 dots per inch

Figure 9.12 Work backwards from the size of your print to find out whether your image has enough pixels.

started with a scan, maybe you can go back and scan at a higher resolution. Otherwise, your image-editing program can create extra pixels by interpolation (see page 26):

1. Go back to the **Resize** or **Image size** dialogue box.
2. Enter the desired resolution (if you've deselected **Resample image**, reselect it now).
3. Enter the desired print size.
4. The program works out how many pixels you need.
5. Click **OK** to make it 'invent' new pixels to bulk up your file.

Interpolation isn't a perfect solution, but it's better than printing your image at a very low resolution. Sharpen the image after resizing to redefine the edges (see page 127).

Excessively high resolutions aren't normally a problem, although they can slow down your printer. If things are getting out of hand, follow the instructions above. At Step 3, the program will realise you have more pixels than you need. When you click **OK** at Step 4, it'll slim down the file. Remember, though, that once the pixels are gone, they're gone for good.

Choosing the right format
When you're printing photographs directly from your image-editing program, you don't have to worry about the file format. However, you might decide to transfer an image to your desktop publishing program, or give it to someone else to print. In these circumstances, you need to save the file in a format most programs can understand. The best option is the TIFF format.

'Resampling' is a general term for adjusting the number of pixels in an image, either by throwing some out or by interpolation.

If you're e-mailing an image to someone specifically so they can print it, you have to compromise. Prepare the image as if you were going to print it yourself, then save it as a JPEG. Don't overdo the compression – the loss of quality is more apparent in printed images than on the screen. You should end up with a file that isn't too enormous to transmit over the internet, but has enough pixels to print well.

Sharing images online

Sending images by e-mail

Using album websites

Creating your own web pages

There's a good chance that you bought your digital camera or scanner specifically so you could share pictures online. E-mailing photographs to friends or displaying them on a website is quick, convenient, and cheap. You can even claim you're doing your bit for the environment by using less paper.

Sending images by e-mail

E-mail enables you to whiz pictures all round the world. Announcing your new baby? A photograph says so much more than the traditional 'weight: 8lb 3oz'. Meeting an old friend? Send them a snapshot so they know how much you've changed. Just keeping in touch? Even day-to-day correspondence benefits from the addition of pictures (Figure 10.1).

Most people like receiving photographs. However, your friends won't thank you for sending images that don't fit on their screen, or can't be displayed, or take forever to download. Before you dash off a message, go back to Chapter 9 and check that your photographs are:

- the right size
- saved in the correct format
- compressed so they'll download quickly.

Sending a picture
To send a picture by e-mail, you 'attach' it to a message. The image file bumps along behind your text, like a trailer being towed behind your car. When the message gets to the recipient, he can unhitch the file and save it on to his hard disk.

Figure 10.1 Don't just tell people what you've seen – show them.

To send a picture to a friend:

1. Create a new e-mail message.
2. Add the address, subject and message text.
3. Look for a button or menu option that lets you attach a file (Figure 10.2).
4. Find and select your file (Figure 10.3). To attach several files from the same folder, hold down **Ctrl** as you click to select them.

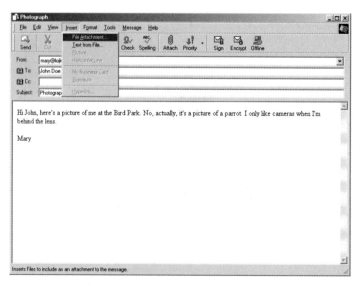

Figure 10.2 To attach an image to an Outlook Express message, click the **Attach** button or select **Insert**, then **File Attachment**.

5. Click **Attach** or **OK** to add the files to your message.

6. Repeat Steps 3, 4, and 5 if you want to attach a file from another folder.

7. Send the message as you would normally.

It's also possible to create e-mail messages that are like little web pages, with the pictures embedded in the text. However, not everyone can receive this kind of message, so it's better to send your pictures as separate files.

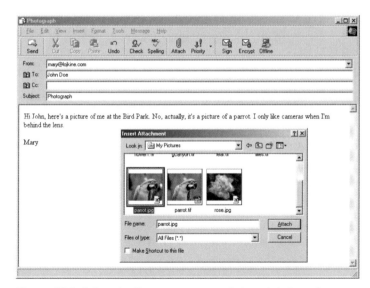

Figure 10.3 Select the file you want to send, then click **Attach**.

Receiving a picture

Receiving pictures isn't difficult, because they just arrive in your Inbox. You might notice that your mail is downloading more slowly than usual. When it arrives, you'll realise someone has sent you a picture – or some sort of file, anyway. Most programs use an icon (for example, a paperclip) to indicate that a message has an attachment, but you can't tell what you've got until you open the message.

Most e-mail programs automatically display any pictures at the end of the associated message. If yours doesn't, you may be able to tell it to – check the Help file.

Sometimes you'll want to save an image on to your hard disk as a separate file. For example, you might want to keep the image but not the message, or load the file into an image editor. To do this:

1. Open the message with the attached file.
2. Look for a menu option that lets you save attachments. Alternatively, right-click on the icon for the attached file, or the picture itself. Select **Save As** or **Save Picture As** from the pop-up menu (Figure 10.4).
3. Select the correct folder (Figure 10.5).
4. Check that the file has a meaningful name.
5. Click **Save**.

Troubleshooting

If you don't have problems with regular messages, you're unlikely to have difficulty with images. Very occasionally, something may go wrong.

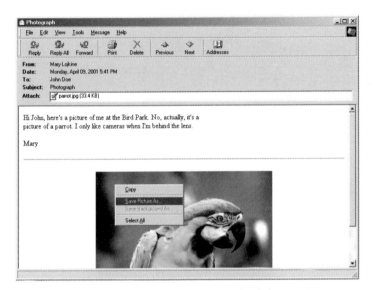

Figure 10.4 To save an attached image, try right-clicking on it.

Problem: Your message bounces back, ending up in your own Inbox.

Things to check: Was the address correct? Did you send a very large file? Most people have a volume (size) limit on their mailbox, and you may have exceeded it. Try sending a smaller version of the image.

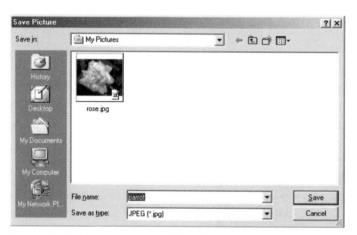

Figure 10.5 Select the correct folder, check the filename and click **Save**.

Problem: Your message arrives, but the recipient can't open the image file.

Things to check: Did you use the correct image format? Does the filename have the correct ending – for example, .jpg for a JPEG? If so, there's a small possibility that your file encountered the electronic equivalent of turbulence and has become corrupted. Try sending it again. If it still doesn't work, you may have an encoding problem. When you send a file, your e-mail program converts it into a format mail systems can handle. Most programs use the MIME (Multipurpose Internet Mail Extensions) system. However, older programs may use other systems, such as Uuencode and BinHex. You may be able to solve the problem by telling your program to use a different encoding system.

Using album websites

E-mail is great when you want to share a few images with a few other people. When you want many more people to be able to view your images, it's more convenient to put your photographs on a website and give everyone the address.

The simplest way to put your photographs on the web is to use an album site. These sites specialise in storing and displaying digital images. You are allocated storage space for your files, which can be organised into albums for different events or subjects (Figure 10.6). Albums can be kept private, shared with selected friends, or made public.

Figure 10.6 PhotoBox (www.photobox.co.uk/) lets you store your photographs and share them online.

The advantage of using an album site is that you don't have to learn how to create web pages; all the technical details are taken care of by the site. It's also possible to restrict access to your pictures. You can share photographs of your children with friends, without exposing them to the entire internet-using world. Many album sites offer printing services, enabling you to turn your digital images into true photographic prints (see page 217). Some sites charge a monthly fee, but there are plenty that don't.

To use an album service, you must first register and create an account. This involves entering a few personal details and selecting a password so you can access your private area of the website. You can then upload your image files as follows:

1. Enter your user name and password to log on to the site.
2. Look for a link that lets you 'Add a photo' or 'Upload photos'.
3. Clicking the link takes you to the upload page. You'll be prompted to enter the location of the file on your hard disk. Click the **Browse** button to find it.
4. Fill in any other details that are requested (Figure 10.7).
5. Click the **Upload** button to copy your file to the album site. This takes a few seconds – or minutes, for a large file.
6. The image is added to your album (Figure 10.8).

If you only want to share your images online, upload small versions of the images so you don't use up your storage space too quickly. If you want to have an image printed, upload a larger version.

You should be able to e-mail your friends with instructions for viewing your pictures. If the site has a printing service, they'll be able to order their own reprints. This is great if you've had a big family event such as a wedding – everyone can order (and pay for!) their own copies of the best photographs. Some sites also let you add captions to your images, display them as a slide show, and turn them into electronic postcards (Figure 10.9).

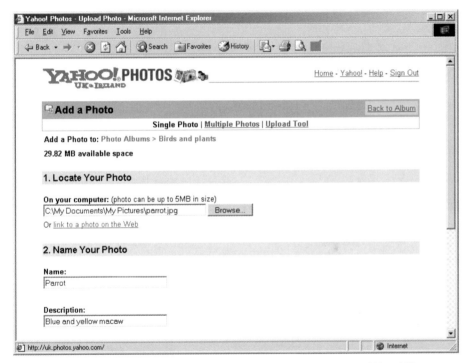

Figure 10.7 Follow the on-screen instructions to upload a photograph to Yahoo! Photos (uk.photos.yahoo.com/).

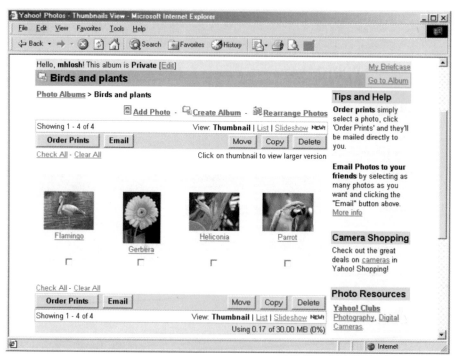

Figure 10.8 Yahoo! Photos displays a small version of each image in your album. Click a small image to see a larger version.

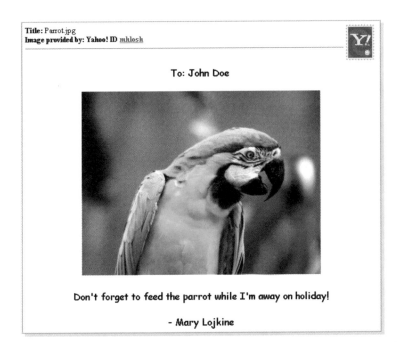

Figure 10.9 E-cards are a fun way to communicate.

Creating your own web pages

For complete control over the display of your images, you'll need to create your own website.

If you use a modern web-design program, you needn't concern yourself with the minutiae of HTML (HyperText Markup Language), the language used to create web pages. Many web-design programs work much like word processors – you simply use the formatting tools to create the effect you want.

Organising your files

There are three things to sort out before you start designing. First, where are you going to put your web pages? They have to be stored on a computer that's permanently connected to the internet, so other people can access them whenever they want. Your internet service provider (ISP) probably gives you some 'web space' as part of your account. It's basically a folder on one of its computers that you can use to store files.

Second, you need to organise your files. A web page might look like a single document, but it's normally constructed from several files. The text is stored in an HTML file, along with all the formatting instructions. The images are all stored in separate files, usually as JPEGs. When a web browser downloads the page, it fetches the text file and checks for references to pictures. It then fetches the picture files and drops them into place.

When you're designing a web page, you store all the files on your hard disk. Once the page is complete, you copy them to your web space. It's very important that you use the same filing system in both places, so you need to think ahead:

1. For a small website, create a new folder in My Documents called, say, 'website'.

2. Within that folder, create a subfolder called 'images'.

3. Move all your image files into 'images'.

4. When you create a web page, save it into 'website'.

5. When you have finished designing your pages, copy all the files from 'website' to your web space.

6. Within your web space, create a new folder called 'images'.

7. Copy all the files from the 'images' folder on your hard disk to the 'images' folder within your web space.

Most computers on the internet can differentiate between upper-case and lower-case letters, so they think Image.jpg and image.jpg are two completely different files. It's best to use lower-case characters for everything, including folder names, to avoid mistakes and confusion. Don't use spaces or other strange characters.

The reason you have to be so meticulous about the names and locations of your files is that HTML uses relative references. When you add a picture to a web page, all you're really adding is an instruction that tells web browsers how to find the image file, *based on the location of the page*. It says something like, 'Hey, you know where this page came from. Go back to that folder, then look in the subfolder called "images". Fetch file "xyz" and add it to this page.' If you change the names of your files, or move them around, the instructions in the pages will get out of date, and web browsers won't be able to find your images. Decide on a filing system before you begin designing, and stick with it.

Finally, make sure your images are the right size, saved in the right format, and compressed (see page 154).

Adding an image
Once you've got everything organised, actually adding your images to a web page is straightforward:

1. Run your web-design program, create a new web page, and save it.
2. Enter your text, then move the cursor to the position where the image should appear.
3. Double-check that your image is in the correct folder.
4. Look for a button or menu option that lets you insert an image (Figure 10.10).
5. Find the image file and click **Open** or **OK**.
6. Click **OK** again to add the image to your page (Figure 10.11).

Formatting your images

Images on web pages behave like small chunks of text. You can format them in much the same way.

- To make a column of pictures down the page, start a new paragraph after each one.
- To make a row of pictures across the page, put them all in the same paragraph (Figure 10.12).
- To centre or right-align an image, select it (usually by clicking on it) and use the buttons that let you align text.

Some formatting options are only relevant for images. To apply them, click an image to select it, then look for an Image Properties option. Try right-clicking on the image – this option often appears on the pop-up menu. In some programs, image properties are automatically displayed on a toolbar when you select the image.

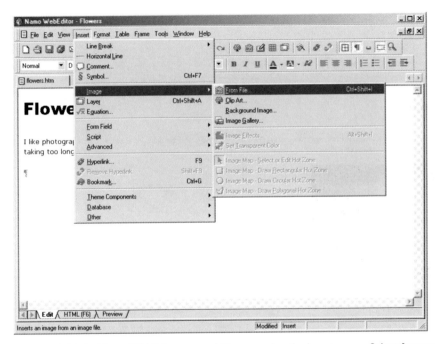

Figure 10.10 In Namo WebEditor, you add images using the Insert menu. Select **Image**, then **From File**.

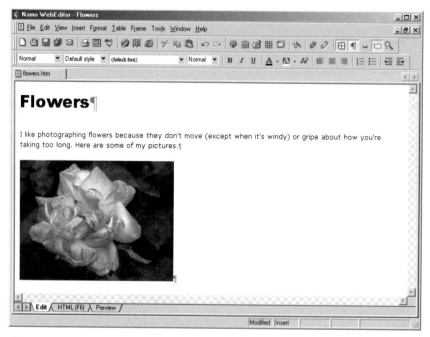

Figure 10.11 The inserted image appears on your page.

- ALT (alternative) text appears while an image is being downloaded. It also pops up if you 'hover' the mouse over your image, without clicking (Figure 10.13). It's useful for people whose web browsers can't display pictures, so they know what they're missing.

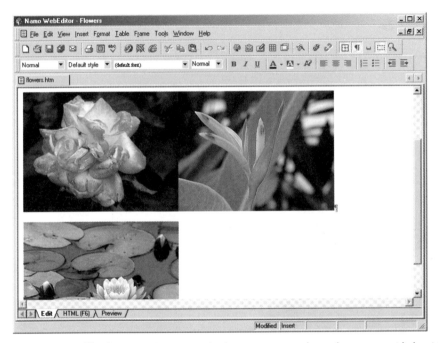

Figure 10.12 The first two pictures are in the same paragraph, so they appear side by side. The third picture is in a new paragraph.

■ If you have text alongside an image, you can align it with the top of the image, the centre or the bottom.

Flowers

I like photographing flowers because they don't move (except when it's windy) or gripe about how you're taking too long. Here are some of my pictures.

Pink and yellow rose

Figure 10.13 ALT text appears when you hold the mouse pointer over the image.

- You can specify the height and width of the image. This is a good idea, because images can take a while to download. If your web browser knows how big the image will be, it can display the text, leaving a 'hole' of the correct size for the image.

- Margins increase the space around (and between) images. You can also add a coloured border (to remove it, set the thickness to 0) (Figure 10.14).

Clickable images

An image can be the anchor for a 'hyperlink' (a link to another web page, or another part of the same page). When you click on it, you are taken to the page at the other end of the link. To link from an image:

1. Click on the image to select it.

2. Look for a button or menu option that lets you add a hyperlink.

3. If you are linking to one of your own pages, select the file from your hard disk (Figure 10.15). If you are linking to a page on another website, fill in the full address, including the http://.

4. Click **OK** to create the link.

When you link from an image, most web browsers automatically add a blue border. To prevent this, set the border thickness to 0 (see the section, Formatting your images, above).

Web page buttons are nothing more than small image files that are linked to other pages. If you want to make photographic buttons, remember that they'll be quite small. It's best to start with simple images that have bold shapes and colours.

*Don't use the **Height** and **Width** settings to resize an image. If you make it bigger, the quality will suffer. If you make it smaller, your web browser has to download the full-size file, then shrink it. Resize the image in your image editor instead.*

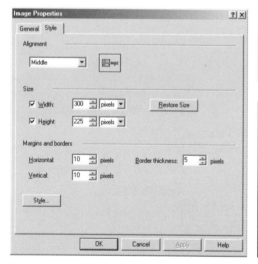

This water lily was a beautiful shape and colour.

Figure 10.14 These settings (a) align the text with the middle of the water lily image, increase the margins and add a border (b).

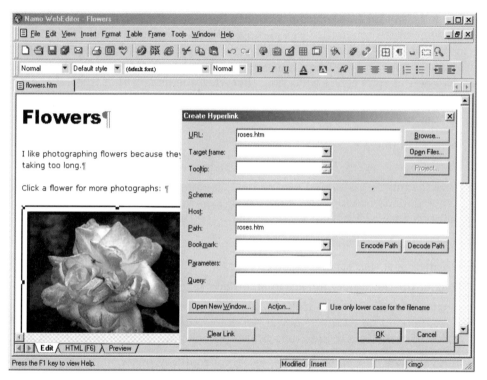

Another reason for linking from an image file is to create an online gallery. You don't want to put too many large photographs on one page, because they'll take a long time to download. A better option is to create a page that displays small versions of your images, then link each one to a larger picture. People can get an overview of your entire collection, then view the images that interest them.

To make a gallery, you need to produce small 'thumbnail' versions of your image files:

1. Open each file in your image editor.
2. Resize it so it is, say, 60 pixels wide (or high, for a vertical image).
3. Save the image, *giving it a new name*. For example, if you started off with an image called rose.jpg, you might save it as rose_t.jpg. The _t on the end makes it easy to work out which image is the thumbnail.

Now you can design your gallery:

1. Create a new web page.
2. Add all the thumbnail images in an orderly fashion.
3. Turn each image into a link. Instead of making the link point to another page, make it point to the larger version of the image. You may need to set **Files of type:** to **All files** to locate your image files (Figure 10.16).

When you click on one of the images on your gallery page, your web browser downloads and displays the larger version. To return to the gallery, click the **Back** button (Figure 10.17).

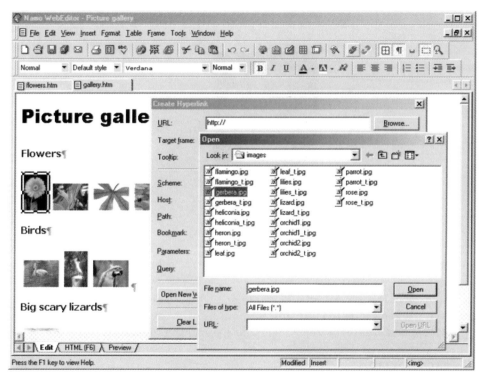

Figure 10.16 You can link to another image file as well as to web pages.

Figure 10.17 When you click on an image in the gallery (a), your browser loads the larger version (b).

Even a page of thumbnail images can take a while to download. As your gallery grows, it's a good idea to split the thumbnails over several pages. Divide them up by topic and create an index page that lists all the topics.

Background images

Bored with white backgrounds for your web pages? You can use an image instead. Web browsers will 'tile' it, repeating it as many times as is necessary to fill the window.

Background images should be very pale so people can still read your text (Figure 10.18). To achieve this, open the image in your image editor, decrease the contrast and increase the brightness – dramatically.

To install your backdrop, look for a menu option that lets you set the **Page Properties** or **Document Properties**. You'll get a dialogue box that lets you specify a background image (among other things).

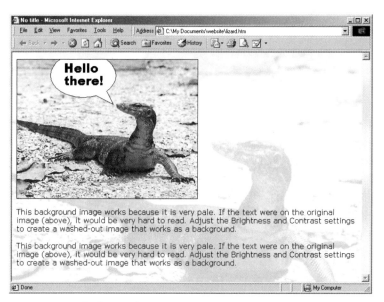

Figure 10.18 Background images should be very pale and washed out.

Choosing a printer

Is editing your images dishonest? Maybe. But is a photograph of 15 people with bright red pupils an accurate depiction of your Christmas party?

However much you pride yourself on being a free-as-air digital photographer, using no film, no chemicals and no paper, there'll come a time when you want to print your images. There's no substitute for a physical print that you can pass round or hang on your wall.

If you're scanning images so you can edit them digitally, you'll certainly want a printer. What's the point in correcting colours and editing out flaws if the final, perfect image can only be viewed on your computer? The output from a modern printer can be almost indistinguishable from a conventional photographic print. If your friends don't go round inspecting everything with a magnifying glass, à la Sherlock Holmes, they may never realise that your digital darkroom has played its part.

To get the best out of your image files, you need a printer designed specifically for printing photographs (Figure 11.1). That's not to say you can't print your images on a general-purpose printer. You can, and you may be happy with the results. However, this chapter focuses on printers that are optimised for printing photographs. Most can also print text, although not as quickly or cheaply as printers designed for churning out documents. A few only print images.

How do photo printers work?

Most photo printers use inkjet technology. A printhead is cranked backwards and forwards across the paper, spraying ink as it goes. The head consists of tanks of liquid ink, plus a mechanism that forces the ink through fine nozzles. Some printers use heat to push the ink out of the nozzles, while others spray it electromechanically. Either way, dots of ink are deposited on your paper.

Figure 11.1 Do your images justice with a photo-quality printer such as Hewlett-Packard's DeskJet 990cxi.

Colour inkjets normally use four or six shades of ink. Other colours are produced by overlapping the dots or printing patterns that, from a normal viewing distance, blend together into an intermediate shade (see page 32). Most printers can vary the size of the dots, so you get very small dots in light-coloured areas and larger ones where the colour is more intense.

Some photo printers use alternative technologies that produce dot-free prints (see Other types of printer, below).

In theory, 'photo-quality' output should be as clear, crisp and colourful as a photograph. In practice, treat this term with scepticism. Manufacturers attach the photo-quality tag to printers whose photo output is 'good enough'.

Choosing an inkjet printer

Photo printers cost more than general-purpose inkjets, so you want to be sure you're buying the right one. There are eight features to consider:

- resolution
- number of colours
- carriage width
- consumables
- connection
- software
- extras
- performance.

Resolution

Ah, resolution. Where would you be without it? With inkjet printers, remember that it takes several image dots to produce each image dot. If you want to print at 300 dpi – and you do, for photo-quality output – you need a printer that's capable of around 1200 dpi.

Like scanners, printers have two resolutions, a horizontal one and a vertical one (see page 96). Manufacturers focus on the horizontal resolution, which is usually higher than the vertical one. The effective resolution lies somewhere between the two.

Some companies produce 1200 dpi printers, while others offer 1440 dpi. The difference is historical and has little effect on the output. You'll also come across printers that operate at 2400 and 2880 dpi (Figure 11.2). On its own, the extra resolution is unimportant, because 1200 and 1440 dpi printers print as much detail as the naked eye can see. The top-of-the-range printers may be more advanced in other ways, but you won't benefit from the extra dots.

Once you get to 1200 dpi, the ability of the printer to size and place the droplets precisely becomes as important as the resolution. The easiest way to assess this is by examining test prints (see Performance on page 213).

Figure 11.2 Epson's Stylus Photo 890 has a top resolution of **2880** × 720 dpi.

Number of colours

Inkjet printers can use three, four or six inks. A three-colour printer uses cyan, magenta and yellow inks. A four-colour one adds black ink, and a six-colour one also has light cyan and light magenta inks.

Three-colour printers are cheap, but the output is nasty. The three inks should combine to create black, but in reality you get dark brown. If you want to print text, you have to replace the three-colour ink cartridge with a black one.

Four-colour printers are more common and much better. They usually take two ink cartridges: one containing the three coloured inks, and a separate one with the black. This arrangement lets you replace the black cartridge more frequently if you're also printing text documents. When one of the three colours runs out, you have to throw out the entire colour cartridge, sacrificing what's left of the other two. Printers that take four separate ink cartridges are more economical, but this feature is uncommon.

The extra inks in a six-colour printer improve the reproduction of skies and pale-coloured skin (Figure 11.3). Instead of printing a few, well-spaced dots of regular ink, the printer lays down lots of closely spaced dots of pale ink. This makes the dots less obvious, so light-coloured areas of your photographs look smoother. Some four-colour printers achieve a similar effect by enabling you to replace the regular cyan and magenta inks with lighter versions.

Carriage width

Standard printers accept A4 paper (21.0×29.7 cm), plus anything smaller. Wide-carriage printers are half as wide again, enabling them to print on A3 paper (29.7×42.0 cm) (Figure 11.4). They also cost half as much again. This is

Figure 11.3 Canon's S800 uses cyan, light cyan, magenta, light magenta, yellow and black inks.

aggravating, because a large part of the difference is longer pieces of plastic. You're really paying for the fact that sales of wide-carriage printers are lower.

If you're thinking about a wide-carriage printer, be aware that the paper and ink costs of a top-quality A3 print are substantial (see Consumables, below). While the prospect of printing your own posters is attractive, it might make more sense to use a printing service (see Professional printing on page 217) for occasional big prints.

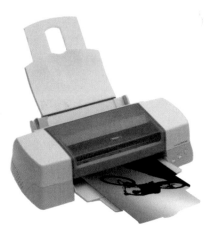

Figure 11.4 Epson's Stylus Photo 1290 is the wide-carriage version of the Photo 890 shown in Figure 11.3.

Consumables

Photo printers are voracious beasts that consume expensive supplies without pause, so it's worth considering the cost of their upkeep.

Manufacturers always say their printers work best with their own inks and papers. This is true. When you're spitting out droplets that contain as little as four picolitres of ink (four millionths of a millionth of a litre), the chemistry of the ink, and the paper it lands on, need to be just right. An inkjet printer is designed as a complete system: the ink, the printhead, the drive mechanism and the paper work together to give you the best possible output.

It's also true that manufacturers make a good chunk of their profits from consumables, so they aren't going to encourage you to use anyone else's products. Papers from other companies can be much cheaper and won't harm your printer. Alternative inks might, but many people use them without problems.

Ink cartridges cost too much and don't last long enough. Check the prices before you buy your printer, and work out how many photographs you can print with each one. Most manufacturers quote a cartridge life somewhere in their brochure, although their estimates tend to be optimistic.

The lifespan of your prints is also an issue. Inkjet prints fade over time (then again, so do conventional photographs). Some inks are guaranteed lightfast for ten, twenty or even one hundred years, when used with the correct paper, but most are not. Hang on to your image files so you can reprint them in the future, if necessary.

Paper comes in four grades: cheap photocopier bond, cheapish coated paper, expensive glossy paper and wallet-emptying glossy film. You can print photographs on copier bond, but it's a waste of your expensive ink. Coated paper gives better results without causing you too much pain at the checkout. The coating prevents the ink from spreading, keeping your dots neat and your edges sharp. It's a good compromise when you want a print, but don't need it to be as detailed or shiny as a photograph. For true photo-quality output, you have to find the money for the top-of-the-range papers. They're available in A3 and A4 sheets, or sized for standard snapshots.

Speciality papers include card, sheets of stickers, overhead-projector transparencies, matt papers for your more 'arty' images, transfer paper that lets you iron your images on to T-shirts, and even cloth. Again, these work best with the manufacturer's own inks. You should also check that they're compatible with your printer.

Connection

Some printers connect to a parallel port, some to a USB port, and some to either. The parallel port has been used for printers since the dawn of the personal computer. You'll even see it referred to as the 'printer port'. It's still a good choice, assuming you aren't already using it for another device, such as a scanner or Zip drive. If you are, you may be able to connect the printer to an extra port on the other device. This doesn't always work, though – some printers prefer to be connected directly to a computer.

USB ports are newer and faster than parallel ports. However, the speed difference isn't a big deal for printing, where the speed of the printer tends to be the limiting factor. It is important if your printer has a built-in memory-card reader (see Extras, below), because you'll want to transfer large amounts of data from the printer to the computer.

For reasons that are lost in the mists of time, you won't get a printer cable with your printer. Normally an enterprising salesperson will point out that this 'optional extra' is, in fact, essential (Figure 11.5).

Software

Although you print from your image editor (or any other program), you still need some software to control the printer. The printer driver acts as a go-between, turning the data from your image editor into something the printer can understand. It also enables you to set printer-specific options. For example, the ideal amount of ink to apply depends on the paper, so you need to tell the printer what's in the paper tray.

Printer manufacturers usually throw in some extra software, such as a basic image editor. By the time you get to buying a photo printer, you might already

Figure 11.5 You'll need either a parallel cable (a) or a USB cable (b) to connect the printer to your computer.

have received an image-editing program with your digital camera, and another one with your scanner, and maybe you didn't like either of them, so you've been out and bought something else. A fourth image editor isn't much of a bonus.

The freebies that are worth having are the ones more directly related to printing. For example, you might get a program that makes it easy to print banners, or rearranges your images so they fit on speciality papers, or generates index prints (Figure 11.6). Read the small print on the back of the box to find out what's on offer.

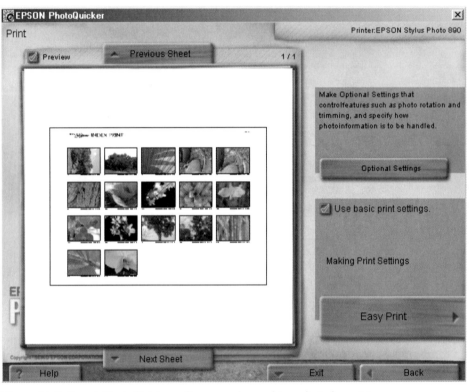

Figure 11.6 Epson's PhotoQuicker software can be used to make index prints.

Extras

All other things being equal, there are a few extra features that might affect your purchasing decision.

Some printers can handle rolls of paper as well as cut sheets. The paper is supported on a spindle (or 'roll holder') at the back and pulled into the printer as required (see Figure 11.2). Roll holders are handy when you're printing panoramic images or banners. Printing on to paper from a roll can also be cheaper than using sheets.

There are several printers with built-in memory-card readers (see page 62) (Figure 11.7). These make it easy to transfer images to your computer. In some cases you can also print directly from the memory card. You won't save much, if anything, on the combined price of a regular printer and a card reader, but you'll only have to connect one device to your computer, rather than two. Check that the reader accepts the memory cards used by your digital camera – you may need an adaptor, which will push up the price.

Canon makes scanning cartridges that can be slotted into some of its printers, in place of the printhead (Figure 11.8). They enable you to scan material that's flat enough to be passed through the printer.

Performance

One way to find a 'good' printer is to look at sample output. Larger retailers, and those that specialise in digital imaging, should have a selection of print-outs from popular models. Find out what type of paper each image is printed on and make sure you're comparing like with like.

Figure 11.7 Hewlett Packard's PhotoSmart printers have slots for CompactFlash and SmartMedia cards.

Figure 11.8 Canon's S800 printer (Figure 11.3) accepts an optional scanning cartridge that turns it into a 600×600 dpi scanner.

When you're reading reviews, concentrate on the features that actually matter to you. Photography magazines often obsess about the ability (or inability, more commonly) of inkjet printers to print black-and-white photographs. This is important if you're interested in black-and-white photography, but of no interest otherwise. Likewise, if you're buying an inkjet printer specifically to handle photographs, you won't care how quickly or neatly it prints text.

Reviews may also mention speed. Don't get excited: all photo printers are mind-numbingly slow. Think minutes per print, not prints per minute.

Other types of printer

The versatility of colour inkjets makes them the most popular type of photo printer. However, there are alternatives. Most are more specialised than inkjets and can't be used for printing text.

Dye-sublimation printers use solid inks (Figure 11.9). The printhead heats the ink, turning it into a gas and transferring it on to the paper. By controlling the heating element, different amounts of each colour can be applied. Because the ink hits the paper as a gas, the colours can be mixed, and there are no discrete dots. Special paper is required to absorb the gaseous inks.

Dye-subs typically have a resolution of 300 dpi (which is sufficient – unlike inkjets, they print one dot per image pixel). Many consumer models only accept one size of paper, usually around 6×4 inches. In other words, you can print standard photographs, but nothing else. Prints have a glossy, waxy finish.

Inkjet printers often struggle with black-and-white images, adding a colour cast of some sort. The best solution is to use ink cartridges specially formulated for black-and-white printing. These have various shades of grey in place of the coloured inks.

Figure 11.9 Olympus' P-400 is a dye-sublimation printer that accepts A4 paper (a). Sony's DPP-SV55 is more typical, producing snapshot-sized prints (b).

Thermal autochrome printers don't use ink (Figure 11.10). Instead, the colours are contained in the paper. When it is heated, the cyan, yellow and magenta pigments are released, producing your image. The printer then fixes the image using ultraviolet light. As with dye-subs, resolution is around 300 dpi and prints are about the same size as standard photographs.

Figure 11.10 Fujifilm's FinePix Printer NX-500 uses thermal autochrome technology.

Professional printing

Although it's nice to have your own printer, it isn't essential. Another option is to find a one-hour photo lab that offers digital processing. These labs use machines that can accept image files as well as rolls of film.

When it's processing film, a digital mini lab scans each frame and uses a built-in computer to decide how to print it. For example, if the image is underexposed, the computer will make it lighter. The data is transferred on to photographic paper using a laser or an array of LEDs (light-emitting diodes). When you give the machine an image file, it skips the scanning stage and simply prints your data. From a user's point of view, it's straightforward: you hand over your memory card, then pop back later to collect your prints.

All the usual concerns about image resolution apply and you'll need 300 dpi files for the best results. Most machines are set up to accept files in the JPEG format, although some can handle other types of file – check with the operator. If you're dubious about handing over your expensive memory card, copy your files on to a disk.

If your high street photo lab hasn't gone high-tech, you can find similar services online (Figure 11.11). You submit your images by e-mail, via a website or using special software, pay by credit card, and receive your prints by post. These services are aimed at digital photographers, so you don't have to explain

Figure 11.11 PhotoBox (www.photobox.co.uk/) offers an online print service.

yourself to someone who'd really rather you'd walked in with a roll of film. You're more likely to be offered print sizes that suit digital images, such as 6 × 4.5 inches rather than 6 × 4, and you'll probably pay less. The only downside is that you'll have to wait longer for your prints.

The great thing about professional printing is that as long as you have enough pixels in your image file, the output is indistinguishable from a conventional photograph. You can also have a lot of fun with edited images. It looks like a photograph, it feels like a photograph...so where did that flying saucer come from?!

Decisions, decisions

When you're buying a printer specifically to print photographs, you must ask yourself two important questions: how good is the output, and how much will each photograph cost?

The best way to find out how different printers perform is to look at sample print-outs. You don't often get a chance to test a digital camera or scanner before you buy, but with printers you can get a reasonable idea of what to expect. Shop around until you find a dealer with a collection of sample print-outs and see how they compare.

If you are enormously wealthy, you can ignore the cost question. Otherwise, give it some thought. Digital imaging is a low-cost hobby until you start purchasing specialist inks and papers, whereupon it can rapidly become an expensive one.

Printing images

12

Printing from your image editor

Printing from DTP programs

Ideas for projects

Some programs complicate matters by letting you resize an image as you print it. This should not affect the file – it's a temporary override that's useful for one-off prints in odd sizes. Note, though, that your image may not be printed at the optimum resolution.

Printing is easy: you hit the **Print** button and see what happens. Or maybe not. When you're using expensive inks and papers, and waiting several minutes for each print-out to emerge, you don't want to experiment. This chapter explains how to adjust your settings to get the best possible results.

Printing from your image editor

When you want a straightforward photograph to frame, or to send to someone, the best option is to print it from your image editor.

Checking the size and resolution

Chapter 9 explains how to adjust the size and resolution of your image file so it will print well. Your image editor should automatically use the current settings when you print the image. For example, if you've specified a width of 15 cm, a height of 10 cm and a resolution of 300 dpi, that's what you should get.

It's important to check these settings when you're printing an image from a digital camera. Your software may give it a default resolution of 72 dpi, turning a 1600 × 1200-pixel file into a massive but low-quality 22 × 17-inch print (Figure 12.1). Changing the resolution to 300 dpi brings the size down to a more reasonable 5.3 × 4 inches.

Choosing the right settings

If you select **Print** and click **OK**, your image editor shrugs its shoulders and uses your printer's default settings – which may be fine, or completely inappropriate. Getting things right is a two-step process: you need to set up your printer, and then you need to decide, each time you print, whether to override the default settings.

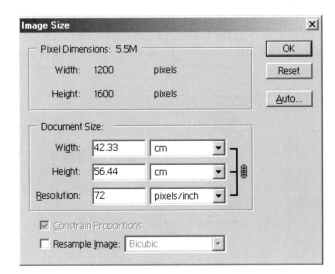 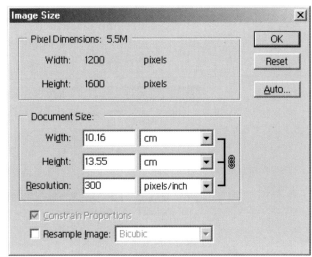

Figure 12.1 You really don't want your printed image to be this big (a). Fixing the resolution (b) solves the problem.

Start by checking your printer's default settings:

1. Click on the **Start** button and select **Settings**, then **Printers**.

2. Right-click on the icon for your printer. Select **Properties** from the pop-up menu.

3. Work through the dialogue box, checking all the settings and correcting them if necessary (Figure 12.2).

The options vary from one printer to the next, but you should be able to set the size and orientation of the paper (normally **A4** and **Portrait**). You can also specify the type of paper. This is important, because it affects the amount of ink that is laid down.

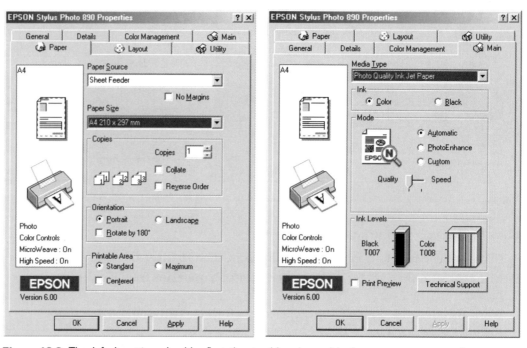

Figure 12.2 The default settings should reflect the size (a) and type (b) of paper you use most often.

Plain paper absorbs ink, enabling it to spread. The paper also gets wet and may 'cockle' (wrinkle) if too much ink is applied. Coated and glossy papers are much less absorbent, so the ink stays on the surface and dries more quickly, producing a sharper print. It will also be brighter, because more ink can be applied.

You'll probably want to print on several different types of paper, depending on the job in hand. Select the one you use most often. You may also be able to select operating modes that emphasise speed, image quality or economical use of ink. All these options can be overridden on a job-by-job basis, so you aren't bound by the decisions you make now. Just choose settings that will do for most of your prints.

When you're ready to print an image, make your last-minute adjustments:

1. Load your paper into the printer.

2. Go to your image editor's **File** menu and select **Print** (or click the **Print** button, if it has one).

3. If you have more than one printer, check that the correct one is selected.

4. Set the number of copies you want.

5. Click the **Setup** button (if there isn't one, skip to the next step).

6. Check the paper size and orientation, and correct them if necessary.

7. Click **Properties**.

8. Check that the right type of paper is selected (Figure 12.3).

9. Click **OK** until you return to the Print dialogue box.

10. Click **OK** once more to print.

A 'portrait' page is taller than it is wide. A 'landscape' page is turned on its side, so it's wider than it is tall. Text documents are usually printed in the portrait orientation, but you'll often want to use landscape for images.

If you change the paper type in Step 8, the new setting only applies until you close your image editor.

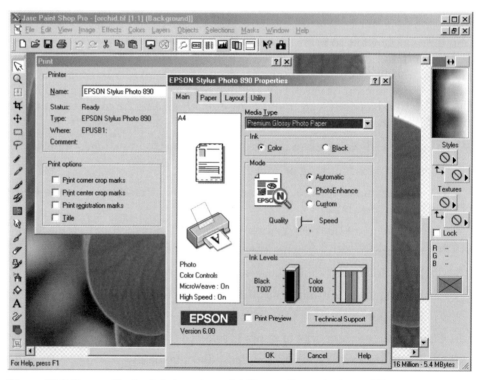

Figure 12.3 To override the default settings, click **Properties** and select a different paper type.

Adjusting colours

Once your print-out emerges, compare it to the image on your screen. Are the colours the same? If they aren't, your problem is that monitors and printers make colours in different ways (see page 30). Some fine-tuning is required to get the two devices in sync.

Some colours are difficult to print with standard inks, such as bright greens and some shades of orange. If your mismatches are confined to these colours, there isn't much you can do.

More expensive papers have a right side and a wrong side. Print on the whiter, shinier side.

More commonly, you'll find that all the colours are slightly off. You can either adjust your monitor or edit your images to compensate. To adjust your monitor:

1. Find a photograph with a good range of colours.
2. Print it out on glossy paper.
3. Adjust the brightness and contrast of the monitor until the screen image matches the printed one.
4. If there's still a difference, see if you can change the colour temperature of the monitor. Lower temperatures give you more red, hotter temperatures more blue.

The alternative is to work out a standard procedure for adjusting your images. The idea is to make the image look slightly wrong on the screen, to allow for the changes that occur when you print it:

1. Create a test sheet containing nine images: one that looks right on your screen, and eight more that you've made slightly darker, lighter, redder, pinker, bluer, more cyan, greener and more yellow (Figure 12.4).

2. Print the test sheet on glossy paper.

3. Compare the printed images to the one on the screen. By seeing which one comes closest, you can work out that you need to add, say, a hint of red to each photograph just before you print it.

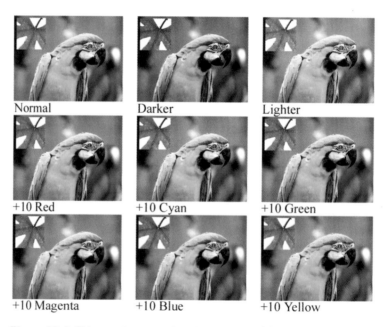

Normal	Darker	Lighter
+10 Red	+10 Cyan	+10 Green
+10 Magenta	+10 Blue	+10 Yellow

Figure 12.4 This test sheet contains nine versions of the image, each treated slightly differently.

Professional colour-matching systems create profiles for both devices, then automatically adjust your images as they move from monitor to printer. Even then, consistent colour is difficult to achieve. Simple things such as changing the lighting around the monitor can throw everything out.

Making the most of your paper
Glossy photo papers are expensive, so you want to use them economically. Do your draft and day-to-day printing on cheaper papers, and save the pricey ones for special projects.

You don't want to print a single 6 × 4-inch image in the middle of an A4 sheet, because you'll waste all the paper round the edges. One option is to use sheets that are sized specially for photographs. Sometimes they have perforated edges, so you can tear off the unprinted borders (Figure 12.5). These miniature sheets are very convenient, especially if you're working with scans. If you're using a digital camera, your images may be too square (see page 48). Crop them to the right shape before you print.

The problem with miniature sheets is that you pay for the convenience. A more economical solution is to print several images on an A4 sheet. Some image-editing programs can arrange the images for you (Figure 12.6), or you can use a desktop publishing program to lay them out yourself (see Printing from DTP programs, below). Use a steel ruler and a craft knife to separate your prints.

A third option is to use paper from a roll, assuming your printer supports this (see page 213).

Figure 12.5 Photo-size sheets with perforated edges are convenient but pricey.

Figure 12.6 Paint Shop Pro lets you arrange several images on each sheet of paper.

Printing from DTP programs

Transferring your images to a desktop publishing (DTP) program gives you complete control over their placement on the page. It's also easy to add borders, captions and notes. You can combine pictures with text to create a family newsletter to send out at Christmas, or to make your own cards, calendars, leaflets or posters (Figure 12.7).

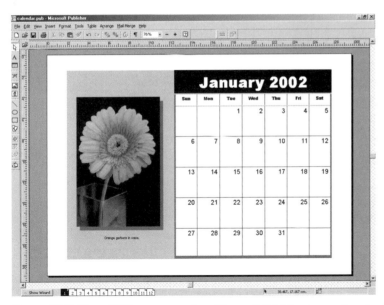

Figure 12.7 Use a DTP program such as Microsoft Publisher to create calendars.

Some image-editing programs also have templates for cards and stationery (Figure 12.8). You drop your photo into a professionally designed frame, hit the **Print** button, sign your card and send it off. Templates make life easy, but sometimes they are so complicated and colourful that your photograph seems like an afterthought. If you want something simple, or something with a lot of text, or you fancy flexing your creative muscles, use a DTP program instead.

When you want to use an image in a DTP document, save it as a TIFF file. All the usual concerns about resolution apply (see page 168). It's best to design your document, leaving a space for the photograph, then size the image file accordingly. It's particularly important to get the sizes right when you're creating a document with several pictures, such as a leaflet or newsletter. If all your image files are too large, your DTP document will be way too large, making it difficult to work on.

Ideas for projects

Not sure what to do with all the image files that are cluttering up your hard disk? Here are some suggestions.

Cards and postcards
Blank cards are always useful. It's hard to go wrong with flowers or scenery, or you can scour the local junk shops and create an interesting still-life. 'Arty' filters that make your image look like a painting or drawing can cover up a multitude of photographic sins (Figure 12.9).

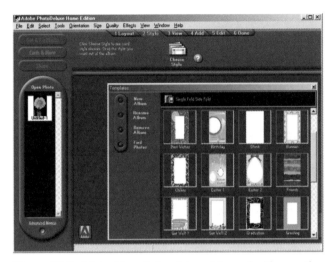

Figure 12.8 Adobe PhotoDeluxe's templates make life easy, if you can find one that complements your photograph.

It's also fun to make one-off cards for specific people or events. Friend just passed her driving test? Use your photo-editing skills to put her behind the wheel of a Porsche – or a beat-up old wreck, depending on your sense of humour. Try adding speech bubbles to snapshots from holidays or parties, too.

Be careful when you're printing on card. If it's too heavy, your printer may not be able to pull it though. Consult the manual for advice, or use the manufacturer's own card. Some sell packs containing prefolded cards and matching envelopes.

Figure 12.9 Use lightweight card to make greetings cards or invitations.

Calendars

A calendar is a good way to show off your photographs. Calendars also make good gifts, although they can be expensive to produce. Add up the cost of 12 sheets of glossy paper, plus an extra one for the cover, plus ink, plus binding, and you'll probably find you can buy a calendar more cheaply. One solution is to rein in your ambitions and use a cheaper grade of paper. Another is to put two or three months on each page – but then you can't use as many photographs.

There are a couple of options for binding your calendar. You can fold all the pages in half and sew or staple them in the centre (get a long-arm stapler from an office supplies catalogue). Alternatively, take the pages to a copy shop and get the staff to wire-bind them across the top.

Posters

When you're trying to sell something via the office noticeboard, a picture will catch the eye of prospective purchasers and get them interested (Figure 12.10). Likewise, 'Come to the office party, we all had a great time last year' isn't half as effective as a photograph of people dancing on tables in a pub or restaurant.

You can also turn your photographs into full-size posters to hang on the wall. This is a job for a professional printing service (see page 217), which will be able to handle much larger sheets of paper than your desktop printer. You'll need a largish image file, but don't bother aiming for the 300 dpi normally associated with printing. You'll be viewing the image from further away, so you can get away with 100–150 dpi.

Figure 12.10 A poster with a picture is more likely to catch someone's eye.

Newsletters

Annual newsletters enclosed with Christmas cards seem to be a fact of modern life. Make them more appealing by adding a few pictures, so people can see how much the children have grown and how much weight/hair you've lost/gained. You don't have to wait until Christmas, either. Pictures liven up a letter at any time of the year, and including them in the document is cheaper than ordering reprints of photos (Figure 12.11).

Use a word processor or desktop publishing program to produce your newsletter. You could even set it out like a newspaper, with articles about specific events and contributions from all the family.

Figure 12.11 If a picture is worth a thousand words, this is a very long letter.

Laminated cards

Try printing out credit-card-sized photographs and asking your local copy shop to laminate them. You can use two photographs back to back, or put useful information such as contact details on the back. Wallet-sized calendars are another possibility (Figure 12.12).

Figure 12.12 Try laminating a small photograph to the back of a calendar.

Stickers and labels

Personalised stickers are great for kids (Figure 12.13). Glossy paper is available with a self-adhesive backing, either plain or pre-cut to give you a number of stickers. With the pre-cut sheets, lining up your images over the stickers can be tricky. Make a test print on plain paper to check the placement.

You can also make labels for almost anything, including CDs, videos, school books, folders, and even jars of jam.

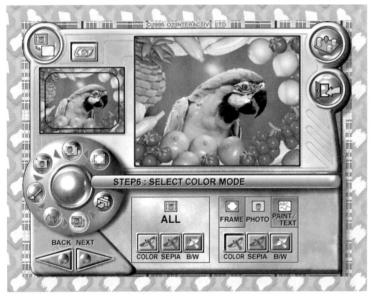 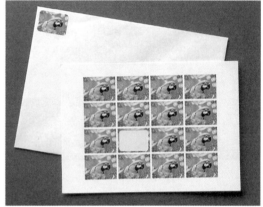

Figure 12.13 Epson's Print Adventure software (a) lets you make funky personalised stickers (b).

T-shirts

Iron-on transfer paper lets you apply your photographs to T-shirts and other fabric items (Figure 12.14). Normally you print on it at a low resolution – typically 360 dpi, which translates to an image resolution of around 120 dpi – so bold, simple images work best. Ironing the back of the paper bonds the inks on to the fabric, enabling them to withstand gentle washing.

Remember that you'll need to reverse your design before you print it, or it'll come out backwards. Use white or pale-coloured fabrics for the best results. White areas are created by not printing anything, so they end up the same colour as the fabric. Also, the inks aren't thick enough to cover a dark background.

Figure 12.14 Use iron-on transfer paper to apply photographs to your chest.

Mouse mats, placemats, coasters and mugs

Professional printing services can put your images on to various items that make novel gifts. How about putting your smiling face on a mouse mat for your boss, with the words 'Promote me' emblazoned across the top? Too blatant? Perhaps a mug featuring a photograph of his or her favourite golf course would be better. Photo gifts are unique and personal, but still have a professional feel (Figure 12.15).

Figure 12.15 The ultimate accessory for your digital darkroom: a photographic mouse mat.

Glossary

24-bit colour Another term for *True Color*.

Album site A *website* that specialises in displaying people's photographs.

All-in-one device A device that enables you to scan, copy, fax and print.

Aperture Camera lenses have a diaphragm that can be opened and closed to control the amount of light hitting the *sensor*. The hole in the middle is the aperture.

Attachment A file attached to an *e-mail*.

Bitmap See *BMP*.

BMP (BitMaP) The *image format* used for Windows *wallpaper*.

CCD (Charge-Coupled Device) A type of *sensor*.

CD writer A device that records data on to a CD, creating a *CD-ROM*.

CD-ROM A CD that contains computer data rather than music.

CIS (Contact Image Sensor) A type of *sensor* used in *scanners*.

Clone To copy *pixels* from one part of an image to another.

CMOS (Complementary Metal-Oxide Semi-conductor) A type of *sensor*.

CMYK (Cyan, Magenta, Yellow, Black) The system used to mix colours in printed documents.

Colour depth The property of a *scanner* that determines how many colours it can perceive.

Colour matching The process of calibrating a *scanner*, a monitor and a printer so they deliver the same colours.

CompactFlash A type of *memory card*.

Composite image An image created from two or more photographs.

Compression A way of condensing the information in an image file, so that less storage space is required.

Cutout An irregular-shaped image with no background.

Digital camera A camera that records images as computer files. It uses a *sensor* and a *memory card* instead of film.

Digital mini lab A photo-processing machine that scans each frame of film and prints it digitally.

DPI (Dots Per Inch) The normal measure for *resolution*.

DTP (DeskTop Publishing) Using a personal computer to prepare documents that contain both text and pictures.

Dye-sublimation printer A printer that applies heat to solid inks, transferring them on to the paper as a gas. Often shortened to dye-sub.

E-mail (electronic mail). A system that enables people to exchange messages across the *internet*.

Exposure Taking a picture involves exposing the camera's *sensor* to light. The amount of light that reaches it – the exposure – depends on the *shutter speed* and *aperture*.

Feather To soften the edge of a selection, by making some *pixels* semi-transparent.

Film scanner A *scanner* designed specially for handling *transparencies*.

Filter In image-editing, a tool that sharpens or softens an image, or applies a special effect.

Focal length Property of a lens that determines how much of a scene you can see and how close your subject seems to be.

Gaussian blur A *filter* that makes images less sharp.

GIF (Graphics Interchange Format) An *image format* used on the *web*.

High Color An operating mode that enables a computer to display over 65 000 colours.

Histogram A plot of the brightness of the *pixels* in a image.

HTML (HyperText Markup Language) The language used to create *websites*.

Hyperlink (link) A connection between two *web* pages. Clicking the link on the first page takes you to the second one.

Image editor A computer program that enables you to edit photographs.

Image format A set of rules for storing the information in a digital image.

Inkjet printer A printer that sprays liquid inks on to the paper.

Internet A global network that connects millions of computers, enabling people to contact each other and access vast quantities of information.

Interpolation A process that adds *pixels* to an image file, by averaging the ones that are already present.

JPEG (Joint Picture Experts Group) The *image format* used for sending photographs by *e-mail* and displaying them on the *world wide web*. Also abbreviated to JPG.

Landscape In printing, a page that is wider than it is tall.

Lasso A tool that lets you select irregular shapes.

Layers The image-editing equivalent of sheets of acetate. Layers enable you to stack up several images to create a collage or *composite image*.

LCD (Liquid Crystal Display) A type of display screen.

Link See *hyperlink*.

Macro A mode that enables a camera to focus on subjects that are very close to the lens.

Magic Wand A tool that selects *pixels* of the same or similar colours.

Megapixel One million *pixels*. Think of a square 1000 pixels wide by 1000 pixels high.

Memory card A small card used to store computer data.

MIME (Multi-purpose Internet Mail Extensions) A set of rules for converting files into a format that *e-mail* systems can handle.

Moiré Interference patterns that appear when you scan printed material, such as pictures from magazines.

Parallel port A socket on the back of the computer that enables you to connect other devices to it. It's most commonly used for printers.

Picture CD A Kodak service that turns a roll of film into a set of prints and a *CD-ROM* containing digital versions of the pictures.

Pixel One of the small coloured squares that makes up a computer image. Short for 'picture element', and otherwise known as a dot.

Portrait In printing, a page that is taller than it is wide.

PPI (Pixels Per Inch) See *DPI*.

Redeye The red pupils that are common in pictures taken using flash.

Resampling A general term for adjusting the number of *pixels* in an image.

Resolution The number of *pixels* in an image, measured on a per-inch or per-image basis.

RGB (Red, Green, Blue) The system used to mix colours on the screen.

Scanner A device that examines ('scans') photographs and drawings, producing a computer version of the image.

SCSI (Small Systems Computer Interface) A system for connecting devices to computers. It isn't standard on PCs.

Sensor In a *digital camera* or *scanner*, the component that turns light into computer data.

Serial port A socket on the back of the computer that enables you to connect other devices to it.

Shutter speed The amount of time for which light is allowed to hit the camera's *sensor*, forming an image.

SLR (Single-Lens Reflex) A type of camera where the viewfinder enables you to look through the lens.

SmartMedia A type of *memory card*.

Template A professionally designed document that you can customise.

Thermal autochrome printer A printer that uses heat-sensitive paper that contains coloured pigments.

Thumbnail A miniature, preview version of an image file.

TIFF (Tagged Image File Format) An *image format* widely used in *DTP*. Also abbreviated to TIF.

Transparency An item that light can pass through, such as a slide or negative.

True Color An operating mode that enables a computer to display up to 16.7 million colours.

TWAIN driver A piece of software that enables other programs to communicate with a *scanner*.

Unsharp Mask A *filter* that makes images sharper.

USB (Universal Serial Bus) A system for connecting devices such as scanners and printers to a computer.

VGA (Video Graphics Array) A *digital camera* or monitor *resolution* of 640 × 480 pixels.

Wallpaper An image displayed on your computer's desktop.

Web See *World wide web*.

Web browser A computer program used for viewing *web* pages.

Webcam A primitive *digital camera* that only works when it's connected to a computer.

Website A group of *web* pages that belong to a person or organisation, or cover a particular topic.

Wide-carriage printer A printer that accepts A3 paper.

World wide web An information service on the *internet*. The web consists of millions of magazine-style pages, connected together by *hyperlinks*.

Zoom lens A lens with a variable *focal length*.

Appendix

Company websites

To find out more about the products mentioned in this book, visit the company websites listed below. The inclusion of a product as an example should not be considered an endorsement. Follow the advice in Chapters 3, 5, 7 and 11 to choose the camera, scanner, image editor and/or printer that is right for you.

Adobe
Image-editing software
www.adobe.co.uk/

Agfa
Digital cameras, scanners
www.agfa.co.uk/

Canon
Digital cameras, scanners, inkjet
    printers
www.canon.co.uk/

Epson
Digital cameras, scanners, inkjet
    and dye-sub printers
www.epson.co.uk/

Fujifilm
Digital cameras, thermal autochrome
    printers
www.fujifilm.co.uk/

Hewlett-Packard
Digital cameras, scanners,
    CD writers, inkjet printers
www.hp.com/uk/

IBM
Microdrive
www.ibm.com/

Iomega
CD writers, Zip drives
www.iomega-europe.com/

Jasc
Image-editing software
www.jasc.com/

Kodak
Picture CD, digital cameras
www.kodak.co.uk/

Logitech
Webcams
www.logitech.com/

Microsoft
Internet, web-design and DTP
  software
www.microsoft.com/

Microtech
Memory cards, card readers
www.microtechint.com/

Namo
Web-design software
www.namo.com/

Nikon
Digital cameras, film scanners
www.nikon.co.uk/

Olympus
Digital cameras, dye-sub printers
www.olympus.co.uk/

PhotoBox
Album site, printing service
www.photobox.co.uk/

SanDisk
Memory cards
www.sandisk.com/

Sony
Digital cameras, dye-sub printers
www.sony.co.uk/

UMAX
Scanners
www.umax.co.uk/

Yahoo! Photos
Album site, printing service
uk.photos.yahoo.com/

Index